Monologues from Shakespeare's First Folio for Any Gender:
The Histories

The Applause Shakespeare Monologue Series

T0346480

Monologues from Shakespeare's First Folio for Any Gender:
The Histories

Compilation and Commentary by
Neil Freeman

Edited by
Paul Sugarman

APPLAUSE
THEATRE & CINEMA BOOKS
Guilford, Connecticut

APPLAUSE
THEATRE & CINEMA BOOKS

An imprint of Globe Pequot, the trade division of
The Rowman & Littlefield Publishing Group, Inc.
4501 Forbes Blvd., Ste. 200
Lanham, MD 20706
www.rowman.com

Distributed by NATIONAL BOOK NETWORK

Library of Congress Cataloging-in-Publication Data available

Library of Congress Control Number: 2021944379

ISBN 978-1-4930-5678-1 (paperback)
ISBN 978-1-4930-5679-8 (ebook)

♾™ The paper used in this publication meets the minimum requirements of
American National Standard for Information Sciences—Permanence of Paper for
Printed Library Materials, ANSI/NISO Z39.48-1992

Dedication

Although Neil Freeman passed to that "undiscovered country" in 2015, his work continues to lead students and actors to a deeper understanding of Shakespeare's plays. With the exception of Shakespeare's words (and my humble foreword), the entirety of the material within these pages is Neil's. May these editions serve as a lasting legacy to a life of dedicated scholarship, and a great passion for Shakespeare.

Contents

Foreword 11

Preface and Brief Background 15

Introduction 19

How these texts work 27

Exeter, *The First Part of Henry the Sixt* 33

Captaine, *The First Part of Henry the Sixt* 37

Lucie, *The First Part of Henry the Sixt* 41

Salisbury, *The Second Part of Henry the Sixt* 45

Hume, *The Second Part of Henry the Sixt* 49

Salisbury, *The Second Part of Henry the Sixt* 53

Jack Cade, *The Second Part of Henry the Sixt* 57

Jack Cade, *The Second Part of Henry the Sixt* 61

Messenger, *The Third Part of Henry the Sixt* 65

Son, *The Third Part of Henry the Sixt* 69

Father, *The Third Part of Henry the Sixt* 73

King Henry, *The Third Part of Henry the Sixt* *77*

Clifford, *The Third Part of Henry the Sixt* *81*

King Henry, *The Third Part of Henry the Sixt* *85*

King Henry, *The Third Part of Henry the Sixt* *89*

2 Murtherer, *The Tragedy of Richard the Third* *93*

3 Citizen, *The Tragedy of Richard the Third* *97*

Scrivener, *The Tragedy of Richard the Third* *101*

Buckingham, *The Tragedy of Richard the Third* *105*

Tyrrel, *The Tragedy of Richard the Third* *109*

Buckingham, *The Tragedy of Richard the Third* *113*

Chattylion, *The Life and Death of King John* *117*

French Herald, *The Life and Death of King John* *121*

English Herald, *The Life and Death of King John* *121*

Arthur, *The Life and Death of King John* *125*

Arthur, *The Life and Death of King John* *129*

Captaine, *The Life and Death of King Richard the Second* *133*

Gardiner, *The Life and Death of King Richard the Second* *137*

Richard, *The Life and Death of King Richard the Second* *141*

Sir Richard Vernon, *The First Part of Henry the Fourth* *145*

Chief Justice, *The Second Part of Henry the Fourth* *149*

Boy, *The Life of Henry the Fift*............................*153*

Mountjoy, *The Life of Henry the Fift* *157*

Boy, *The Life of Henry the Fift*............................*161*

Herald, *The Life of Henry the Fift* *165*

Chorus, *The Life of Henry the Fift*.........................*169*

Griffith, *The Life of King Henry the Eight* *173*

Bibliography *179*

Appendix 1: Guide to the Early Texts *183*

Appendix 2: Words, Words, Words........................*184*

Appendix 3: The Pattern of Magic *187*

Acknowledgments.......................................*189*

Author Bio *190*

FOREWORD

Paul Sugarman

Monologues from Shakespeare's First Folio presents the work of Neil Freeman, longtime champion of Shakespeare's First Folio, whose groundbreaking explorations into how first printings offered insights to the text in rehearsals, stage and in the classroom. This work continued with *Once More Unto the Speech Dear Friends: Monologues from Shakespeare's First Folio with Modern Text Versions for Comparison* where Neil collected over 900 monologues divided between the Comedy, History and Tragedy Published by Applause in three masterful volumes which present the original First Folio text side by side with the modern, edited version of the text. These volumes provide a massive amount of material and information. However both the literary scope, and the literal size of these volumes can be intimidating and overwhelming. This series' intent is to make the work more accessible by taking material from the encyclopediac original volumes and presenting it in an accessible workbook format.

To better focus the work for actors and students the texts are contrasted side by side with introductory notes before and commentary after to aid the exploration of the text. By comparing modern and First Folio printings, Neil points the way to gain new insights into Shakespeare's text. Editors over the centuries have "corrected" and updated the texts to make them "accessible," or "grammatically correct." In doing so they have lost vital clues and information that Shakespeare placed there for his actors. With the texts side by side, you can see where and why editors have made changes and what may have been lost in translation.

In addition to being divided into Histories, Comedies, and Tragedies, the original series further breaks down speeches by the character's designated gender, also indicating speeches appropriate for any gender. Drawing from this example, this series breaks down each original volume into four workbooks: speeches for Women of all ages, Younger Men, Older Men and Any Gender. Gender is naturally fluid for Shakespeare's characters since during his time, ALL of the characters were portrayed by males. Contemporary productions of Shakespeare commonly switch character genders (Prospero has become Prospera), in addition to presenting single gender, reverse gender and gender non-specific productions. There are certainly characters and speeches where the gender is immaterial, hence the inclusion of a volume of speeches for Any Gender. This was something that Neil had indicated in the original volumes; we are merely following his example.

The monologues in the book are arranged by play in approximate order of composition, so you get his earliest plays first and can observe how his rhetorical art developed over time. The speeches are then arranged by their order in the play.

Once More Unto the Speech Dear Friends was a culmination of Neil's dedicated efforts to make the First Folio more accessible and available to readers and to illuminate for actors the many clues within the Folio text, as originally published. The material in this book is drawn from that work and retains Neil's British spelling of words (i.e. capitalisation) and his extensive commentary on each speech. Neil went on to continue this work as a master teacher of Shakespeare with another series of Shakespeare editions, his 'rhythm texts' and the ebook that he published on Apple Books, *The Shakespeare Variations.*

Neil published on his own First Folio editions of the plays in modern type which were the basis the Folio Texts series published by Applause of all 36 plays in the First Folio. These individual editions all have extensive notes on the changes that modern editions had made. This material was then combined to create a complete reproduction of the First Folio in modern type, *The Applause First Folio of Shakespeare in Modern Type.* These editions make the First Folio more accessible than ever before. The examples in this book demonstrate how the clues from the First Folio will give insights to understanding and performing these speeches and why it is a worthwhile endeavour to discover the riches in the First Folio.

PREFACE AND BRIEF BACKGROUND TO THE FIRST FOLIO

There has been an enormous change in theatre organisation recent in the last twenty years. While the major large-scale companies have continued to flourish, many small theatre companies have come into being, leading to

- much doubling
- cross gender casting, with many one time male roles now being played legitimately by/as women in updated time-period productions
- young actors being asked to play leading roles at far earlier points in their careers

All this has meant actors should be able to demonstrate enormous flexibility rather than one limited range/style. In turn, this has meant

- a change in audition expectations
- actors are often expected to show more range than ever before
- often several shorter audition speeches are asked for instead of one or two longer ones
- sometimes the initial auditions are conducted in a shorter amount of time

Thus, to stay at the top of the game, the actor needs more knowledge of what makes the play tick, especially since

- early plays demand a different style from the later ones
- the four genres (comedy, history, tragedy, and the peculiar romances) all have different acting/textual requirements
- parts originally written for the older, more experienced actors again require a different approach from those written for the younger

Neil Freeman

ones, as the young roles, especially the female ones, were played by young actors extraordinarily skilled in the arts of rhetoric

There's now much more knowledge of how the original quarto and folio texts can add to the rehearsal exploration/acting and directing process as well as to the final performance.

Each speech is made up of four parts

- a background to the speech, placing it in the context of the play, and offering line length and an approximate timing to help you choose what might be right for any auditioning occasion
- a modern text version of the speech, with the sentence structure clearly delineated side by side with
- a folio version of the speech, where modern texts changes to the capitalization, spelling and sentence structure can be plainly seen
- a commentary explaining the differences between the two texts, and in what way the original setting can offer you more information to explore

Thus if they wish, **beginners** can explore just the background and the modern text version of the speech.

An actor experienced in exploring the Folio can make use of the background and the Folio version of the speech

And those wanting to know as many details as possible and how they could help define the deft stepping stones of the arc of the speech can use all four elements on the page.

The First Folio

(FOR LIST OF CURRENT REPRODUCTIONS SEE BIBLIOGRAPHY

The end of 1623 saw the publication of the justifiably famed First Folio (F1). The single volume, published in a run of approximately 1,000 copies at the princely sum of one pound (a tremendous risk, considering that a single play would sell at no more than six pence, one fortieth of F1's price, and that the annual salary of a schoolmaster was only ten pounds), contained thirty-six plays.

The manuscripts from which each F1 play would be printed came from a variety of sources. Some had already been printed. Some came from the playhouse complete with production details. Some had no theatrical input at all, but were handsomely copied out and easy to read. Some were supposedly very messy, complete with first draft scribbles and crossings out. Yet, as Charlton Hinman, the revered dean of First Folio studies describes F1 in the Introduction to the Norton Facsimile:

> It is of inestimable value for what it is, for what it contains. For here are preserved the masterworks of the man universally recognized as our greatest writer; and preserved, as Ben Jonson realized at the time of the original publication, not for an age but for all time.

WHAT DOES F1 REPRESENT?

- texts prepared for actors who rehearsed three days for a new play and one day for one already in the repertoire
- written in a style (rhetoric incorporating debate) so different from ours (grammatical) that many modern alterations based on grammar (or poetry) have done remarkable harm to the rhetorical/debate quality of the original text and thus to interpretations of characters at key moments of stress.
- written for an acting company the core of which steadily grew older, and whose skills and interests changed markedly over twenty years as well as for an audience whose make-up and interests likewise changed as the company grew more experienced

The whole is based upon supposedly the best documents available at the time, collected by men closest to Shakespeare throughout his career, and brought to a single printing house whose errors are now widely understood - far more than those of some of the printing houses that produced the original quartos.

TEXTUAL SOURCES FOR THE AUDITION SPEECHES

Individual modern editions consulted in the preparation of the Modern Text version of the speeches are listed in the Bibliography under the separate headings 'The Complete Works in Compendium Format' and ' The Complete Works in Separate Individual Volumes.' Most of the modern versions of the speeches are a compilation of several of these texts. However, all modern act, scene and/or line numbers refer the reader to The Riverside Shakespeare, in my opinion still the best of the complete works despite the excellent compendiums that have been published since.

The First Folio versions of the speeches are taken from a variety of already published sources, including not only all the texts listed in the 'Photostatted Reproductions in Compendium Format' section of the Bibliography, but also earlier, individually printed volumes, such as the twentieth century editions published under the collective title *The Facsimiles of Plays from The First Folio of Shakespeare* by Faber & Gwyer, and the nineteenth century editions published on behalf of The New Shakespeare Society.

INTRODUCTION

So, congratulations , you've got an audition, and for a Shakespeare play no less.

You've done all your homework, including, hopefully , reading the whole play to see the full range and development of the character.

You've got an idea of the character, the situation in which you/it finds itself (the given circumstance s); what your/its needs are (objectives/ intentions); and what you intend to do about them (action /tactics).

You've looked up all the unusual words in a good dictionary or glossary; you've turned to a well edited modern edition to find out what some of the more obscure references mean.

And those of you who understand metre and rhythm have worked on the poetic values of the speech, and you are word perfect . . .

. . . and yet it's still not working properly and/or you feel there's more to be gleaned from the text , but you're not sure what that something is or how to go about getting at it; in other words, all is not quite right, yet.

THE KEY QUESTION

What text have you been working with - a good modern text or an 'original' text, that is a copy of one of the first printings of the play?

If it's a modern text, no matter how well edited (and there are some splendid single copy editions available, see the Bibliography for further details), despite all the learned information offered, it's not surprising you feel somewhat at a loss, for there is a huge difference between the original printings (the First Folio, and the individual quartos, see

Appendix 1 for further details) and any text prepared after 1700 right up to the most modern of editions. All the post 1700 texts have been tidied-up for the modern reader to ingest silently, revamped according to the rules of correct grammar, syntax and poetry. However the 'originals' were prepared for actors speaking aloud playing characters often in a great deal of emotional and/or intellectual stress, and were set down on paper according to the very flexible rules of rhetoric and a seemingly very cavalier attitude towards the rules of grammar, and syntax, and spelling, and capitalisation, and even poetry.

Unfortunately, because of the grammatical and syntactical standardisation in place by the early 1700's, many of the quirks and oddities of the origin also have been dismissed as 'accidental' - usually as compositor error either in deciphering the original manuscript, falling prey to their own particular idosyncracies, or not having calculated correctly the amount of space needed to set the text. Modern texts dismiss the possibility that these very quirks and oddities may be by Shakespeare, hearing his characters in as much difficulty as poor Peter Quince is in *A Midsummer Night's Dream* (when he, as the Prologue, terrified and struck down by stage fright, makes a huge grammatical hash in introducing his play 'Pyramus and Thisbe' before the aristocracy, whose acceptance or otherwise, can make or break him)

> If we offend, it is with our good will.
> That you should think, we come not to offend,
> But with good will.
>   To show our simple skill,
> That is the true beginning of our end .
> Consider then, we come but in despite.
> We do not come, as minding to content you ,
> Our true intent is.
>   All for your delight
> We are not here.
>   That you should here repent you,

The Actors are at hand; and by their show,
You shall know all, that you are like to know.

(AMidsummer Night's Dream)

In many other cases in the complete works what was originally printed is equally 'peculiar,' but, unlike Peter Quince , these peculiarities are usually regularised by most modern texts.

However, this series of volumes is based on the belief - as the following will show - that most of these 'peculiarities' resulted from Shakespeare setting down for his actors the stresses, trials, and tribulations the characters are experiencing as they think and speak, and thus are theatrical gold-dust for the actor, director, scholar, teacher, and general reader alike.

THE FIRST ESSENTIAL DIFFERENCE BETWEEN THE TWO TEXTS

THINKING

A **modern** text can show

- the story line
- your character's conflict with the world at large
- your character's conflict with certain individuals within that world

but because of the very way an 'original' text was set, it can show you all this plus one key extra, the very thing that makes big speeches what they are

- the conflict within the character

WHY?

Any good playwright writes about characters in stressful situations who are often in a state of conflict not only with the world around them and the people in that world, but also within themselves. And you probably know from personal experience that when these conflicts occur people do not necessarily utter the most perfect of grammatical/poetic/ syntactic statements, phrases, or sentences. Joy and delight, pain and sorrow often come sweeping through in the way things are said, in the incoherence of the phrases, the running together of normally disassociated ideas, and even in the sounds of the words themselves.

The tremendous advantage of the period in which Shakespeare was setting his plays down on paper and how they first appeared in print was that when characters were rational and in control of self and situation, their phrasing and sentences (and poetic structure) would appear to be quite normal even to a modern eye - but when things were going wrong, so sentences and phrasing (and poetic structure) would become highly erratic. But the Quince type eccentricities are rarely allowed to stand. Sadly, in tidying , most modern texts usually make the text far too clean, thus setting rationality when none originally existed.

THE SECOND ESSENTIAL DIFFERENCE BETWEEN THE TWO TEXTS
SPEAKING, ARGUING, DEBATING

Having discovered what and how you/your character is thinking is only the first stage of the work - you/it then have to speak aloud, in a society that absolutely loved to speak - and not only speak ideas (content) but to speak entertainingly so as to keep listeners enthralled (and this was especially so when you have little content to offer and have to mask it somehow - think of today 's television adverts and political spin doctors as a parallel and you get the picture). Indeed one of the Elizabethan 'how to win an argument' books was very precise about this - George Puttenham, *The Art of English Poesie* (1589).

A: ELIZABETHAN SCHOOLING

All educated classes could debate/argue at the drop of a hat, for both boys (in 'petty-schools') and girls (by books and tutors) were trained in what was known overall as the art of rhetoric, which itself was split into three parts

- first, how to distinguish the real from false appearances/outward show (think of the three caskets in *The Merchant of Venice* where the language on the gold and silver caskets enticingly, and deceptively, seems to offer hopes of great personal rewards that are dashed when the language is carefully explored, whereas once the apparent threat on the lead casket is carefully analysed the reward therein is the greatest that could be hoped for)

- second, how to frame your argument on one of 'three great grounds'; honour/morality; justice/legality; and, when all else fails, expedience/practicality.

- third, how to order and phrase your argument so winsomely that your audience will vote for you no matter how good the opposition - and there were well over two hundred rules and variations by which winning could be achieved, all of which had to be assimilated before a child's education was considered over and done with.

B: THINKING ON YOUR FEET: I.E. THE QUICK, DEFT , RAPID MODIFICATION OF EACH TINY THOUGHT

The Elizabethan/therefore your character/therefore you were also trained to explore and modify your thoughts as you spoke - never would you see a sentence in its entirety and have it perfectly worked out in your mind before you spoke (unless it was a deliberately written, formal public declaration, as with the Officer of the Court in The Winter' s Tale, reading the charges against Hermione). Thus after uttering your very first phrase, you might expand it, or modify it, deny it, change it, and so on throughout the whole sentence and speech.

Neil Freeman

From the poet Samuel Coleridge Taylor there is a wonderful description of how Shakespeare puts thoughts together like "a serpent twisting and untwisting in its own strength," that is, with one thought springing out of the one previous. Treat each new phrase as a fresh unravelling of the serpent's coil. What is discovered (and therefore said) is only revealed as the old coil/phrase disappears revealing a new coil in its place. The new coil is the new thought. The old coil moves/disappears because the previous phrase is finished with as soon as it is spoken.

C: MODERN APPLICATION

It is very rarely we speak dispassionately in our 'real' lives, after all thoughts give rise to feelings, feelings give rise to thoughts, and we usually speak both together - unless

1/ we're trying very hard for some reason to control ourselves and not give ourselves away

2/ or the volcano of emotions within us is so strong that we cannot control ourselves, and feelings swamp thoughts

3/ and sometimes whether deliberately or unconsciously we colour words according to our feelings; the humanity behind the words so revealed is instantly understandable.

D: HOW THE ORIGINAL TEXTS NATURALLY ENHANCE/ UNDERSCORE THIS CONTROL OR RELEASE

The amazing thing about the way all Elizabethan/early Jacobean texts were first set down (the term used to describe the printed words on the page being 'orthography'), is that it was flexible, it allowed for such variations to be automatically set down without fear of grammatical repercussion.

So if Shakespeare heard Juliet's nurse working hard to try to convince Juliet that the Prince's nephew Juliet is being forced to (bigamously) marry, instead of setting the everyday normal

'O he's a lovely gentleman'

which the modern texts HAVE to set, the first printings were permitted to set

'O hee's a Lovely Gentleman'

suggesting that something might be going on inside the Nurse that causes her to release such excessive extra energy.

E: BE CAREFUL

This needs to be stressed very carefully: the orthography doesn't dictate to you/force you to accept exactly what it means. The orthography simply suggests you might want to explore this moment further or more deeply.

In other words, simply because of the flexibility with which the Elizabethans/Shakespeare could set down on paper what they heard in their minds or wanted their listeners to hear, in addition to all the modern acting necessities of character - situation, objective, intention, action, and tactics the original Shakespeare texts offer pointers to where feelings (either emotional or intellectual, or when combined together as passion, both) are also evident.

SUMMARY

BASIC APPROACH TO THE SPEECHES SHOWN BELOW

(after reading the 'background')

1/ first use the modem version shown in the first column: by doing so you can discover

- the basic plot line of what's happening to the character, and
- the first set of conflicts/obstacles impinging on the character as a result of the situation or actions of other characters
- the supposed grammatical and poetical correctnesses of the speech

2/ then you can explore

- any acting techniques you'd apply to any modem soliloquy, including establishing for the character
- the given circumstances of the scene
- their outward state of being (who they are sociologically, etc.)
- their intentions and objectives
- the resultant action and tactics they decide to pursue

3/ when this is complete, turn to the First Folio version of the text, shown on the facing page: this will help you discover and explore

- the precise thinking and debating process so essential to an understanding of any Shakespeare text
- the moments when the text is NOT grammatically or poetically as correct as the modern texts would have you believe, which will in tum help you recognise
- the moments of conflict and struggle stemming from within the character itself
- the sense of fun and enjoyment the Shakespeare language nearly always offers you no matter how dire the situation

4/ should you wish to further explore even more the differences between the two texts, the commentary that follows discusses how the First Folio has been changed, and what those alterations might mean for the human arc of the speech

NOTES ON HOW THESE SPEECHES ARE SET UP

For each of the speeches the first page will include the Background on the speech and other information including number of lines, approximate timing and who is addressed. Then will follow a spread which shows the modern text version on the left and the First Folio version on the right, followed by a page of Commentary.

PROBABLE TIMING: (shown on the Background page before the speeches begin, set below the number of lines) 0.45 = a forty-five second speech

SYMBOLS & ABBREVIATIONS IN THE COMMENTARY AND TEXT

F: the First Folio

mt.: modern texts

F # followed by a number: the number of the sentence under discussion in the First Folio version of the speech, thus F #7 would refer to the seventh sentence

mt. # followed by a numb er: the number of the sentence under discussion in the modern text version of the speech, thus mt. #5 would refer to the fifth sentence

 # /#, (e.g. 3/7): the first number refers to the number of capital letters in the passage under discussion; the second refers to the number of long spellings therein

within a quotation from the speech: / indicates where one verse line ends and a fresh one starts

[ ] : set around words in both texts when Fl sets one word , mt another

{ } : some minor alteration has been made, in a speech built up, where, a word or phrase will be changed, added, or removed

{†} : this symbol shows where a sizeable part of the text is omitted

TERMS FOUND IN THE COMMENTARY
OVERALL

1/ **orthography**: the capitalization, spellings, punctuation of the First Folio
SIGNS OF IMPORTANT DISCOVERIES/ARGUMENTS WITHIN A FIRST FOLIO SPEECH

2/ **major punctuation**: colons and semicolons: since the Shakespeare texts are based so much on the art of debate and argument, the importance of F1 's major punctuation must not be underestimated, for both the semi-colon (;) and colon (:) mark a moment of importance for the character, either for itself, as a moment of discovery or revelation, or as a key point in a discussion, argument or debate that it wishes to impress upon other characters onstage

as a rule of thumb:

a/ the more frequent colon (:) suggests that whatever the power of the point discovered or argued, the character is not side-tracked and can continue with the argument - as such, the colon can be regarded as a **logical** connection

b/ the far less frequent semicolon (;) suggests that because of the power inherent in the point discovered or argued, the character is side-tracked and momentarily loses the argument and falls back into itself or can only continue the argument with great difficulty - as such, the semicolon should be regarded as an **emotional** connection

3/ **surround phrases**: phrase(s) surrounded by major punctuation, or a combination of major punctuation and the end or beginning of a sentence: thus these phrases seem to be of especial importance for both character and speech, well worth exploring as key to the argument made and /or emotions released

DIALOGUE NOT FOUND IN THE FIRST FOLIO

∞ set where modern texts add dialogue from a quarto text which has not been included in Fl

A LOOSE RULE OF THUMB TO THE THINKING PROCESS OF A FIRST FOLIO CHARACTER

1/ mental discipline/**intellect**: a section where capitals dominate suggests that the intellectual reason ing behind what is being spoken or discovered is of more concern than the personal response beneath it

2/ feelings/**emotions**: a section where long spellings dominate suggests that the personal response to what is being spoken or discovered is of more concern than the intellectual reasoning behind it

3/ **passion**: a section where both long spellings and capitals are present in almost equal proportions suggests that both mind and emotion/feelings are inseparable, and thus the character is speaking passionately

SIGNS OF LESS THAN GRAMMATICAL THINKING WITHIN A FIRST FOLIO SPEECH

1/ **onrush**: sometimes thoughts are coming so fast that several topics are joined together as one long sentence suggesting that the F character's mind is working very quickly, or that his/her emotional state is causing some concern: most mod ern texts split such a sentence into several grammatically correct parts (the opening speech of *As You Like It* is a fine example, where F's long 18 line opening sentence is split into six): while the modern texts' resetting may be syntactically correct, the F moment is nowhere near as calm as the revisions suggest

2/ **fast-link**: sometimes F shows thoughts moving so quickly for a character that the connecting punctuation between disparate topics is merely a comma, suggesting that there is virtually no pause in springing from one idea to the next: unfortunately most modern texts rarely allow this to stand, instead replacing the obviously disturbed comma with a grammatical period, once more creating calm that it seems the original texts never intended to show

FIRST FOLIO SIGNS OF WHEN VERBAL GAME PLAYING HAS TO STOP

1/ **non-embellished:** a section with neither capitals nor long spellings suggests that what is being discovered or spoken is so important to the character that there is no time to guss it up with vocal or mental excesses: an unusual moment of self-control

2/ **short sentence:** coming out of a society where debate was second nature, man y of Shakespeare's characters speak in long sentences in which ideas are stated, explored, redefined and summarized all before moving onto the next idea in the argument, discovery or debate: the longer sentence is the sign of a rhetorically trained mind used to public speaking (oratory), but at times an idea or discovery is so startling or inevitable that length is either unnecessary or impossible to maintain : hence the occasional very important short sentence suggests that there is no time for the niceties of oratorical adornment with which to sugar the pill - verbal games are at an end and now the basic core of the issue must be faced

3/ **monosyllabic:** with English being composed of two strands, the polysyllabic (stemming from French, Italian, Latin and Greek), and the monosyllabic (from the Anglo-Saxon), each strand has two distinct functions: the polysyllabic words are often used when there is time for fanciful elaboration and rich description (which could be described as 'excessive rhetoric') while the monosyllabic occur when, literally, there is no other way of putting a basic question or comment - Juliet's "Do you love me? I know thou wilt say aye" is a classic example of both monosyllables and non-embellishment: with monosyllables, only the naked truth is being spoken, nothing is hidden

Monologues from Shakespeare's First Folio for Any Gender: *The Histories*

The First Part of Henry the Sixt

Duke of Exeter

Well didst thou Richard to suppresse thy voice :
4.1.182 - 194

Background: the quarrel between the Houses of Yorke and Lancaster has grown to such heights that King Henry has had to step in to block a request for formal combat between rival supporters. In what (in the next two plays) proves to be an appallingly mistaken attempt to downplay the symbol of which colour rose members of his court wear, Henry has chosen 'red', thus seeming to support Somerset and the Lancastrians. Richard, Duke of Yorke, holder of the white rose, has held his tongue for the moment, for which Exeter, another great-uncle to the King, is thankful.

Style: solo

Where: the English Court, meeting in Paris

To Whom: self and direct audience address

# of Lines: 13

Probable Timing: 0.45 minutes

Take Note: The simple act of modern texts creating two logical sentences from the longer F #1 almost completely wipes out the normally phlegmatic Exeter's very knowledgeable and, here, free-flowing concerns.

Exeter

1 Well didst thou, Richard, to suppress thy voice ;
   For had the passions of thy heart burst out,
   I fear we should have seen decipher'd there
   More rancorous spite, more furious raging broils,
   [Than] yet can be imagin'd or suppos'd .

2 But howsoe'er, no simple man that sees
   This jarring discord of nobility,
   This shouldering of each other in the court,
   This factious bandying of their favorites,
   But [sees] it doth presage some ill event .

3 'Tis much, when sceptres are in children's hands ;
   But more, when envy breeds unkind division:
   There comes the ruin, there begins confusion .

Exeter

1   Well didst thou Richard to suppresse thy voice :
    For had the passions of thy heart burst out,
    I feare we should have seene decipher'd there
    More rancorous spight, more furious raging broyles,
    [Then] yet can be imagin'd or suppos'd :
    But howsoere, no simple man that sees
    This jarring discord of Nobilitie,
    This shouldering of each other in the Court,
    This factious bandying of their Favourites,
    But [that] it doth presage some ill event .

2   'Tis much, when Scepters are in Childrens hands :
    But more, when Envy breeds unkinde devision,
    There comes the ruine, there begins confusion .

- the speed of the first F line (the two added modern grammatical commas) is the first sign that Exeter's normal calm is here highly disturbed

- the first surround phrase explains from where the danger might stem
    " . Well didst thou Richard to suppresse thy voice :"
  while the second explains why
    " . 'Tis much, when Scepters are in Childrens hands :"

- the apparent calm of the virtually non-embellished first F sentence is somewhat undermined by the fact while the new mt. sentence #2 is grammatically correct, the F Exeter moves from the specific (Richard) to the much greater general ('the jarring discord of Nobilitie') without a sentence break – a sure sign that he is disturbed

- it is only as he envisages the potential appalling future (F #2) that his mind and personal feelings begin to break through (3/3)

Captain/Captaine

Thou ominous and fearefull Owle of death,
4.2.15 - 41

Background: speaking on behalf of those within the city of 'Burdeaux', the following is the defiant French response to Talbot who, on behalf of the English besieging army, has demanded 'Open your Citie Gates,/be humble to us, call my Soveraigne yours' least 'Lean Famine, quartering Steele, and climbing Fire,/Who in a moment, eeven with the earth,/Shall lay your stately, and ayre-braving Towers'.

Style: public address

Where: from the walls at the gates of the city

To Whom: the English general Talbot, in front of his army

# of Lines: 27

Probable Timing: 1.25 minutes

Take Note: A combination of the modern texts' creating nine sentences out of F's four, and their inability to reproduce the original orthography cuts out the remarkable control and the sudden loss of it the F Captaine displays.

Captain

1   Thou ominous and fearful owl of death,
    Our nation's terror and their bloody scourge !

2   The period of thy tyranny approacheth .

3   On us thou canst not enter but by death ;
    For I protest we are well fortified,
    And strong enough to issue out and fight .

4   If thou retire, the Dolphin, well appointed,
    Stands with the snares of war to tangle thee .

5   On either hand thee, there are squadrons pitch'd,
    To wall thee from the liberty of flight ;
    And no way canst thou turn thee for redress,
    But death doth front thee with apparent spoil,
    And pale destruction meets thee in the face .

6   Ten thousand French have ta'en the sacrament
    To rive their dangerous artillery
    Upon no Christian soul but English Talbot .

7   Lo, there thou stand'st, a breathing valiant man,
    Of an invincible unconquer'd spirit !

8   This is the latest glory of thy praise
    That I thy enemy [due] thee withal;
    For ere the glass, that now begins to run,
    Finish the process of his sandy hour,
    These eyes, that see thee now well colored,
    Shall see thee withered, bloody, pale, and dead .

    [**Drum afar off**]

9   Hark, hark, the Dolphin's drum, a warning bell,
    Sings heavy music to thy timorous soul,
    And mine shall ring thy dire departure out .

Captaine

1   Thou ominous and fearful Owle of death,
      Our Nations terror, and their bloody scourge,
      The period of thy Tyranny approacheth,
      On us thou canst not enter but by death :
      For I protest we are well fortified,
      And strong enough to issue out and fight .

2   If thou retire, the Dolphin well appointed,
      Stands with the snares of Warre to tangle thee .

3   On either hand thee, there are squadrons pitcht,
      To wall thee from the liberty of Flight ;
      And no way canst thou turne thee for redresse,
      But death doth front thee with apparant spoyle,
      And pale destruction meets thee in the face :
      Ten thousand French have tane the Sacrament,
      To ryve their dangerous Artillerie
      Upon no Christian soule but English Talbot :
      Loe, there thou standst a breathing valiant man
      Of an invincible unconquer'd spirit :
      This is the latest Glorie of thy praise,
      That I thy enemy [dew] thee withall :
      For ere the Glasse that now begins to runne,
      Finish the processe of his sandy houre,
      These eyes that see thee now well coloured,
      Shall see thee withered, bloody, pale, and dead .

                    [**Drum a farre off**]

4   Harke, harke, the Dolphins drumme, a warning bell,
      Sings heavy Musicke to thy timorous soule,
      And mine shall ring thy dire departure out .

- the longer F sentences (#1 split into three by most modern texts; #3 into four) allow for a great build of defiance, with the act itself as important as what is being said

- but it should not be assumed that the speech is simply one long act of braggadocio, for orthographically the F text falls into at least four major parts, each highly revealing of the man beneath the act

- given the circumstances, the opening 10 lines (F sentences #1-#2 and the first two lines of #3) seem very calm: the Captaine's personal feelings are being kept well in check (just 3 long spellings), and though his act and images of defiance are strong, there are only 6 capitalized words - he seems to be handling the situation in exemplary military and diplomatic fashion

- but, once the Captaine points out that there is no escape for Talbot (lines 3-5 of F #3), there comes a three line break in composure where his personal feelings seem to break through (0/3) - and the start of this emotional break is marked by the only (emotional) semicolon in the speech

- then, between the first two colons of F #3, as the Captaine details the numbers and determination of the French forces ranged against Talbot and the English so his intellect (based on pride perhaps?) comes flooding through once more (6/2)

- then, marked by the last two colons of F #3 (and speech), comes a moment of wonderful calm as man to man, soldier to soldier, the Captaine pays Talbot his honourable due ("Loe, there . . ." 1/1)

- finally, as the last seven lines of the speech focus on Talbot's inevitable fate ("For ere the Glasse . . . "), so the Captaine's personal feelings break through (3/10), much more sustained than before

The First Part of
Henry the Sixt

Lucy/Lucie

{I am sent} my Lord, from bought & sold L. Talbot,
between 4.4. 13 -46

Background: with the appalling and ever-growing factionalism between the houses of Yorke and Somerset, soon to lead to the dreadful civil war known simply as 'The War of the Roses', the maintaining and supplying of the English forces in France has become a minor consideration, with each side blaming the other for the continued failures to support the expeditionary forces. Here, Lord Lucie appeals on behalf of Talbot to Somerset, leader of the Lancastrian faction (wearers of the red rose), who, initially blaming Talbot for his 'unheedfull, desperate, wilde adventure', sloughs off blame to the Yorkist side.

Style: one on one in front of a larger group

Where: in France, some distance away from Talbot's forces

To Whom: Somerset, in front of his army and the Captain accompanying Lucie

# of Lines: 22

Probable Timing: 1.25 minutes

Take Note: The one key modern text sentence restructuring (splitting F's #1 into two) suggests that Lucie is in total control as he faces down the fighting warlords. Nothing could be further from the truth.

Background

Lucy

1 {I am sent} my lord, from bought & sold [Lord] Talbot,
   Who, ring'd about with bold adversity,
   Cries out for noble York and Somerset
   To beat assailing death from his weak [legions];
   And whiles the honorable captain there
   Drops bloody sweat from his war-wearied limbs,
   And, in advantage ling'ring looks for rescue,
   You, his false hopes, the trust of England's honor,
   Keep off aloof with worthless emulation .

2 Let not your private discord keep away
   The levied succors that should lend him aid,
   While he renowned noble gentleman
   Yield up his life unto a world of odds.

3 Orleance the Bastard, Charles, Burgundy,
   Alanson, [Reignier], compass him about,
   And Talbot perisheth by your default .

_____

4 The fraud of England, not the force of France,
   Hath now entrapp'd the noble-minded Talbot :
   Never to England shall he bear his life,
   But dies, betray'd to fortune by your strife .

_____

5 {†} If he be dead, brave Talbot, then adieu !

6 His Fame lives in the world, his shame in you .

Lucie

1   {I am sent} my Lord, from bought & sold [L.]Talbot,
     Who ring'd about with bold adversitie,
     Cries out for noble Yorke and Somerset,
     To beate assayling death from his weake [Regions],
     And whiles the honourable Captaine there
     Drops bloody swet from his warre-wearied limbes,
     And in advantage lingring lookes for rescue,
     You his false hopes, the trust of Englands honor,
     Keepe off aloofe with worthlesse emulation :
     Let not your private discord keepe away
     The levied succours that should lend him ayde,
     While he renowned Noble Gentleman
     Yeeld up his life unto a world of oddes .

2   Orleance the Bastard, Charles, Burgundie,
     Alanson, [Reignard], compasse him about,
     And Talbot perisheth by your default .

---

3   The fraud of England, not the force of France,
     Hath now intrapt the Noble-minded Talbot :
     Never to England shall he beare his life,
     But dies betraid to fortune by your strife .

---

4 {†} If he be dead, brave Talbot then adieu,
     His Fame lives in the world .

5   His Shame in you .

- orthographically, there are several clues that Lucie is having great difficulty in maintaining his composure

- the opening three lines of F sentence #1 is as expected - mental control is uppermost as the basic information about which Lucie has come is embarked upon (4/1)

- but then, surprisingly, for the remainder of the sentence intellectual control disappears and his own personal feelings/anguish about the men he is forced to confront comes bursting through (16/5)

- but once his expressions of disgust and pleading for aid for Talbot are complete then the lack of control is also seen where modern texts have decided to create a second sentence (four lines from the end F sentence #1): the onrushing blurt stemming from the F colon suggests that he cannot contain himself as tidily as the modern texts would wish, but that his feelings must out, unchecked, until fully expressed

- he manages to regain intellectual discipline (14/2) for the remainder of the speech (F sentences #2-5)

- however, the cost of this can be seen in the highly ungrammatical F sentence #5 ending the speech, which most modern texts fold into the previous sentence: as originally set, the F blame could not have been more strongly uttered or apportioned – and its effect on Lucie is (grammatically) highly disturbing; the modern restructuring renders the shock of the F moment as much more polite

- there are at least five occasions where modern texts add extra punctuation not set in the original script, all of which has the effect of slowing what F suggested was Lucie's urgency: this can be seen at the start of line 2 of F #1, the start of lines 7-8 in the same sentence, the end of F sentence #3, and the beginning of F sentence #4

The Second Part of Henry the Sixt

Salisbury

Pride went before, Ambition followes him .

1.1.180 - 204

Background: Salisbury, a supporter of the Duke of Yorke, has witnessed the outburst of the 'haughtie Cardinall' against the Lancastrian Gloster, and, following the Cardinall's exit, the immediate power-hungry response of Buckingham (a supporter of the Lancastrian leader Somerset) that 'Or thou, or I Somerset will be Protectors,/Despite Duke Humfrey, or the Cardinall'. Buckingham and Somerset have now left, and Salisbury is talking to Yorke and his supporters.

Style: three-handed scene

Where: the English court

To Whom: Yorke and Salisbury's son Warwicke

# of Lines: 25

Probable Timing: 1.30 minutes

Take Note: As usual, the modern restructuring of F's sentence structure standardises what F sets up as a somewhat troubled speech for a smaller character.

Salisbury

1 Pride went before, ambition follows him .

2 While these do labor for their own preferment,
   Behooves it us to labor for the realm .

3 I never saw but [Humphrey] Duke of [Gloucester]
   Did bear him like a noble gentleman .

4 Oft have I seen the haughty Cardinal,
   More like a soldier [than] a man o'th'church,
   As stout and proud as he were lord of all,
   Swear like a ruffian, and demean himself
   Unlike the ruler of a commonweal .

5 Warwick, my son, the comfort of my age,
   Thy deeds, thy plainness, and thy house-keeping,
   Hath won the greatest favor of the commons,
   Excepting none but good Duke [Humphrey] ;
   And, brother York, thy acts in Ireland,
   In bringing them to civil discipline,
   Thy late exploits done in the heart of France
   When thou were Regent for our sovereign,
   Have made thee fear'd and honor'd of the people ;
   Join we together, for the public good,
   In what we can to bridle and suppress
   The pride of Suffolk and the Cardinal,
   With Somerset's and Buckingham's ambition ;
   And as we may, cherish Duke [Humphrey's] deeds
   While they do tend the profit of the land .

Salisbury

1   Pride went before, Ambition followes him .

2   While these do labour for their owne preferment,
     Behooves it us to labor for the Realme .

3   I never saw but [Humfrey] Duke of [Gloster],
     Did beare him like a Noble Gentleman :
     Oft have I seene the haughty Cardinall .

4   More like a Souldier [then] a man o'th'Church,
     As stout and proud as he were Lord of all,
     Sweare like a Ruffian, and demeane himselfe
     Unlike the Ruler of a Common-weale .

5   Warwicke my sonne, the comfort of my age,
     Thy deeds, thy plainnesse, and thy house-keeping,
     Hath wonne the greatest favour of the Commons,
     Excepting none but good Duke [Humfrey] .

6   And Brother Yorke, thy Acts in Ireland,
     In bringing them to civill Discipline :
     Thy late exploits done in the heart of France,
     When thou were Regent for our Soveraigne,
     Have made thee fear'd and honor'd of the people,
     Joyne we together for the publike good,
     In what we can, to bridle and suppresse
     The pride of Suffolke, and the Cardinall,
     With Somersets and Buckinghams Ambition,
     And as we may, cherish Duke [Humfries] deeds,
     While they do tend the profit of the Land .

- as Salisbury turns his attention to the Cardinall, F sets up a strange non-grammatical moment (the last line of sentence #3) where his first line is interrupted by a full period before continuing his analysis as a new sentence (F #4): this is never set by any modern text (editors arguing that a period was not set in the non-authoritative quarto): however, F's ungrammatical setting suggests that Salisbury needs a long moment before continuing, and that assessing the Cardinall is highly troubling for him

- similarly, in seeking the support of the two men with him for the good of the 'Realme', F's Salisbury takes care to give each the courtesy of one complete sentence (to his son Warwicke, F #5), and then to Yorke, F #6): this suggests great tact and self-control, at least till the long F #6 begins to run away with him: the modern texts jam both together, suggesting less control and more urgency throughout

- the F extra breath-thoughts (marked ,), especially the three in the last sentence, suggest that dealing with Suffolke and the Cardinall will take great care, and even creates in Salisbury some tension or stronger feelings

- as with many smaller characters facing a crisis point, the shifts in thinking energy are often quite marked
    - a/ the opening short sentence neatly summing up Gloster as 'pride' and the Cardinall as 'ambition' is straight to the point and passionate (1/1)
    - b/ while the two line condemnation of F #2 switches quickly to an emotional response (1/3) – distrust and/or dislike perhaps?
    - c/ and then the F #3 assessment of Gloster and the first line of the same for the Cardinall is once more highly intellectual (6/3 in three lines)
    - d/ the full assessment of the Cardinall (F #4) then switches to passion as his feelings for the man are fully expressed (6/5 in four lines), which continues into his addressing his son Warwicke (F #5, 3/5 in four lines – pride perhaps?)
    - e/ and in F's final intellectual appeal to Yorke and description of what will have to be done (16/6 in eleven lines), three of the seven long spellings come in a two line cluster as the first suggestion of 'Joyne we together for the publike good/In what we can, to bridle and suppresse' is voiced

The Second Part of Henry the Sixt

Hume

Hume must make merry with the Duchesse Gold :
1.2.87 - 107

Background: Suffolke's plot depends on catching Elianor red-handed in the act of witchcraft, which, even though she is only using it to decipher the future, can be used to destroy her reputation and earn her banishment, if not death. To that end, his intermediary is Sir John Hume, a priest, who acts as liaison between Elianor ,the witch Marjery Jordan, and the conjurer Roger Bullingbroke. Having verbally seduced Elianor by referring to her as 'your Royall Majesty' and set up a session at which she will be arrested, now alone, Hume explains himself to the audience.

Style: solo

Where: unspecified, but probably the Gloster's private chambers

To Whom: direct audience address

# of Lines: 21

Probable Timing: 1.10 minutes

Take Note: F's faster opening and closing to this speech (one sentence each, not the modern texts' two), plus the very fast switch in its orthographic releases, creates an enormously complex three-scene character: indeed, if Hume were a modern creation, a reader would be justified in asking whether he was on some form of medication, legal or otherwise.

Background

Hume

1   Hume must make merry with the Duchess gold ;
     Marry, and shall .

2   But how now, Sir John Hume ?

3   Seal up your lips, and give no words but mum ;
     The business asketh silent secrecy .

4   Dame [Eleanor] gives gold to bring the witch ;
     Gold cannot come amiss, were she a devil.

5   Yet have I gold flies from another coast -
     I dare not say from the rich Cardinal,
     And from the great and new-made Duke of Suffolk;
     Yet I do find it so ; for, to be plain,
     They, knowing Dame [Eleanor's] aspiring humor,
     Have hired me to under mine the Duchess,
     And buzz these conjurations in her brain.

6   They say, "A crafty knave does need no broker,"
     Yet am I Suffolk and the Cardinal's broker.

7   Hume, if you take not heed, you shall go near
     To call them both a pair of crafty knaves.

8   Well, so it stands ; and thus, I fear, at last,
     Hume's knavery will be the duchess' wrack,
     And her attainture will be Humphrey's fall .

9   Sort how it will, I shall have gold for all .

Hume

1   Hume must make merry with the Duchesse Gold:
Marry and shall: but how now, Sir John Hume?

2   Seale up your Lips, and give no words but Mum,
The businesse asketh silent secrecie.

3   Dame [Elianor] gives Gold, to bring the Witch:
Gold cannot come amisse, were she a Devill.

4   Yet have I gold flyes from another Coast:
I dare not say, from the rich Cardinall,
And from the great and new-made Duke of Suffolke;
Yet I doe finde it so: for to be plaine,
They (knowing Dame [Elianors] aspiring humor,
Have hyred me to under-mine the Duchesse,
And buzze these Conjurations in her brayne.

5   They say, A craftie Knave do's need no Broker,
Yet am I Suffolke and the Cardinalls Broker.

6   Hume, if you take not heed, you shall goe neere
To call them both a payre of craftie Knaves.

7   Well, so it stands: and thus I feare at last,
Humes Knaverie will be the Duchesse Wracke,
And her Attainture, will be Humphreyes fall:
Sort how it will, I shall have Gold for all.

- the many surround phrases clearly illustrate his sole motivation
  - " . Hume must make merry with the Duchesse Gold : /Marry and shall : but how now, Sir John Hume ? "
  - " . Dame Elianor gives Gold, to bring the Witch : /Gold cannot come amisse, were she a Devill . "
  - " . Well, so it stands : "
  - " : Sort how it will, I shall have Gold for all . "

- though capitals are slightly more prevalent than long-spellings (32/24) his switches back and forth are quick and often large scale: in fact there are no fewer than 8 switches in just 21 lines!

  a/ F #1 is highly factual (5/1 in just two lines)

  b/ the need for secrecy (#2) switches to passion (2/2 in just two lines)

  c/ the gold from Elianor is mentally celebrated (3/0 in F #3's first line)

  d/ the passion flows once more as he celebrates the fact of gold coming in from the arch-foes Elianor and Suffolke (7/8 in the last line of F #3 and the first five lines of #4)

  e/ then, at the end of F #4, emotion breaks through once again as Hume mentions he has 'hyred' people for the plot to deceive Elianor (2/4 in the last two lines)

  f/ as he praises himself as a 'craftie Knave' (F #5) his mental joy comes crashing through (6/2 in just two lines)

  g/ then comes an emotional response (glee at his own wit in extending the 'craftie Knave image' to both Elianor and Suffolke ? - 1/3 in 2 lines)

  h/ and passion concludes the speech (6/4 in the four lines of #7) as he offers the thought that he will benefit financially 'Sort how it will'

The Second Part of
Henry the Sixt
Salisbury

Sirs stand apart, the King shall know your/Minde .
3.2.242 - 269

Background: as Salisbury explains, the people at large are fully convinced of Suffolke's complicity in the suspicious death of their beloved Gloster, a man generously disposed towards the common man, and they fear Suffolke's ambition may extend to Henry himself. The top of this speech is triggered by the fact that the irate Warwicke, another Henry loyalist horrified by Gloster's death (whose body has been brought on-stage), has, in the presence of the King, appeared with his sword drawn on Suffolke, who has responded in kind.

Style: essentially a public address to one man, for the benefit of a larger group

Where: the English court in London

To Whom: King Henry, in front of Suffolke, Margaret, Warwicke, Beauford, Somerset, and Attendants

# of Lines: 28

Probable Timing: 1.30 minutes

Take Note: Apart from the first line, the sentence structure of the two texts match. F's orthography highlights some unexpected depths for a speech often dismissed (or even cut) as being of use only as information, spoken by a character often regarded as rather dull.

Salisbury

1   Sirs stand apart, the King shall know your mind
     Dread lord, the commons send you word by me,
     Unless [false] Suffolk straight be done to death,
     Or banished fair England's territories,
     They will by violence tear him from your palace,
     And torture him with grievous ling'ring death.

2   They say, by him the good Duke [Humphrey] died;
     They say, in him they fear your Highness' death;
     And mere instinct of love and loyalty,
     Free from a stubborn opposite intent,
     As being thought to contradict your liking,
     Makes them thus forward in his banishment.

3   They say, in care of your most royal person,
     That if your Highness should intend to sleep,
     And charge that no man should disturb your rest
     In pain of your dislike, or pain of death,
     Yet notwithstanding such a strait edict,
     Were there a serpent seen, with forked tongue,
     That slily glided towards your Majesty,
     It were but necessary you were wak'd,
     [Lest] being suffer'd in that [harmless] slumber,
     The mortal worm might make the sleep eternal.

4   And therefore do they cry, though you forbid,
     That they will guard you, [whe'er] you will, or no,
     From such fell serpents as false Suffolk is;
     With whose envenomed and fatal sting,
     Your loving uncle, twenty times his worth,
     They say is shamefully bereft of life.

Salisbury

1   Sirs stand apart, the King shall know your minde.

2   Dread Lord, the Commons send you word by me,
     Unlesse [Lord] Suffolke straight be done to death,
     Or banished faire Englands Territories,
     They will by violence teare him from your Pallace,
     And torture him with grievous lingring death.

3   They say, by him the good Duke [[Humfrey]] dy'de :
     They say, in him they feare your Highnesse death ;
     And meere instinct of Love and Loyaltie,
     Free from a stubborne opposite intent,
     As being thought to contradict your liking,
     Makes them thus forward in his Banishment.

4   They say, in care of your most Royall Person,
     That if your Highnesse should intend to sleepe,
     And charge, that no man should disturbe your rest,
     In paine of your dislike, or paine of death ;
     Yet notwithstanding such a strait Edict,
     Were there a Serpent seene, with forked Tongue,
     That slyly glyded towards your Majestie,
     It were but necessarie you were wak't :
     [Least] being suffer'd in that [harmefull] slumber,
     The mortall Worme might make the sleepe eternall.

5   And therefore doe they cry, though you forbid,
     That they will guard you, [where] you will, or no,
     From such fell Serpents as false Suffolke is ;
     With whose invenomed and fatall sting,
     Your loving Unckle, twentie times his worth,
     They say is shamefully bereft of life.

- the unusually short opening F sentence has a two-fold advantage:
  - a/ it allows for a far more deliberate and purposeful control of the Commons who are accompanying him
  - b/ it throws into far sharper focus the important statement of F as to why protocol has been broken to the extent of his coming unannounced to make such an amazingly anti-Suffolke demand

  by setting two separate sentences F suggests that Salisbury is in firm control of self and situation – by running the two sentences together, modern texts have both blurred the separate actions, and suggested that the character is not in such self control

- the single surround phrase (F #3) shows exactly what has triggered Salisbury and the Common's fears

  " ; They say, in him they feare your Highnesse death ; "

- the first of the three (emotional) semi-colons emphasise the motive for their actions ('meere instinct of Love and Loyaltie'), while the other two reinforce Salisbury's comparing Suffolke to a 'Serpent'

- Salisbury starts out with the (only to be expected) passion of a loyal subject moved to voice such an amazingly strong request in such powerful language (20/19 in twenty lines making up the first four sentences, with the exception of the last two lines of F #4)

- but, with the equating of Suffolke not just with the death of Gloster but also with a possible attack on Henry himself, thus excusing Salisbury's and the Commons current demand as a perceived need to protect their king, personal feelings finally swamp Salisbury (4/10 in eight lines)

The Second Part of Henry the Sixt

Jack Cade

Up Fish-streete, downe Saint Magnes corner,

4.8.1 – 5 & 20 - 32

Background: the rebel Jack Cade, presenting himself as Mortimer, the rightful heir to the throne (who, though with a legitimate claim, died in prison) having swept through the South-East of England is now wreaking murderous havoc in London itself. The royalists Buckingham and Clifford meet his forces and attempt to appeal to their loyalty by invoking the glorious memories of the time of the much beloved Henry V. The following is how Cade mishandles the situation.

Style: public address, to two opposing monarchists and an unspecified number of his own men

Where: in the streets of London

To Whom: Buckingham, Clifford, and Cade's own rebel forces

# of Lines: 17

Probable Timing: 1.00 minutes

Take Note: F's orthography and minor sentence variations add more depth to an already colourful character.

Cade

1　Up Fish-street ! down Saint [Magnus'] corner !
kill and knock down ! throw them into Thames !
Sound a parley

2　What noise is this I hear ?

3　　　　　　　　　　　　　　Dare any be so bold to sound
retreat or parley when I command them kill ?

4　What, Buckingham and Clifford, are ye so brave ?

5　And you, base peasants, do ye believe him ?

6　　　　　　　　　　　　　　　　　　Will you needs
be hang'd with your pardons about your necks ?

7　　　　　　　　　　　　　　　　　　　　Hath
my sword therefore broke through London gates, that
you should leave me at the White Hart in [Southwark]?

8　I thought ye would never have given [over] these armstill
you had recovered your ancient freedom .

9　　　　　　　　　　　　　　　　　But you are
all recreants and dastards, and delight to live in slavery
to the nobility .

10　　　　　　　　　　　　　Let them break your backs with bur-
thens, take your houses over your heads, ravish your
wives and daughters before your faces .

11　　　　　　　　　　　　　　　　For me, I will
make shift for one ; and so God's curse light upon you
all !

Cade

1   Up Fish-streete, downe Saint [Magnes] corner,
kill and knocke downe, throw them into Thames{:}

Sound a parley

What noise is this I heare ?

2   Dare any be so bold to sound Retreat or Parley
When I command them kill ?

---

3   What Buckingham and Clifford are ye so brave ?

4   And you base Pezants, do ye beleeve him, will you needs
be hang'd with your Pardons about your neckes ?

5   Hath
my sword therefore broke through London gates, that
you should leave me at the White-heart in [Southwarke] .

6   I thought ye would never have given [out] these Armes til
you had recovered your ancient Freedome .

7   But you are
all Recreants and Dastards, and delight to live in slaverie
to the Nobility .

8   Let them breake your backes with bur-
thens, take your houses over your heads, ravish your
Wives and Daughters before your faces .

9   For me, I will
make shift for one, and so Gods Cursse light uppon you
all.

- while the opening two and a half lines of the speech are highly passionate (4/5) they are not plagued by the four exclamation marks that most modern texts have added, thus suggesting that he starts with speed and enjoyment, not just a generalised unfocused yell

- though at the (shaded) end of sentence #1 and all of #2, F switches to irregular verse (6/13/6 syllables - perhaps suggesting that Cade suddenly assumes a public swagger and bravado in facing down a perceived challenge, so as to substantiate his pretend role as the noble John Mortimer, claimant to the throne), most modern texts, arguing white space, maintain the opening prose, with at least one text omitting the Ff phrase 'I heare', claiming it to be compositorial invention

- and surprisingly, given the circumstances of his men abandoning him, the remainder of the speech contains almost twice as many capitals (16) as long-spellings (9)

- with the arrival of the Lordly enemy leaders and Cade's challenge first to them (F #2-3) and then to his men (F #4-5) , he uses a highly intellectual approach (9/3 in six lines), perhaps suggesting his need to argue carefully to get his points across, or, more likely, over-confidence

- but then, in disbelief that his men have changed sides so easily (F #6), passion breaks through again (2/2 in one and a half lines)

- then, as he begins to curse his men out (F #7), intellect momentarily returns (3/0 in one and a half lines)

- and as he finishes the curse, extending it to their families, and vows to seek for his own safety (F's #8-9, ending the speech), so passion breaks through again (4/4)

The Second Part of
Henry the Sixt
Jack Cade

Was ever Feather so lightly blowne too & fro,
4.8.55 - 65

Background: Buckingham and Clifford finally win over Cade's forces, arguing that only their surrender to the King (without any punishment to follow) can protect them from supposed invasion by the French (a highly spurious invention if ever there was one). Thus Cade is forced to flee.

Style: solo, even though surrounded by many from two opposing groups

Where: in the streets of London

To Whom: direct audience address, in the midst of his own men who have just surrendered to the royalist forces

# of Lines: 10

Probable Timing: 0.35 minutes

Take Note: As with Cade's prior speech, F's orthography and minor sentence variations add more depth to an already colourful character.

Cade

1   Was ever feather so lightly blown too & fro
    as this multitude ?

2   The name of Henry the Fift hales them
    to an hundred mischiefs, and makes them leave me de-
    solate .

3   I see them lay their heads together to surprise
    me .

4   My sword make way for me, for here is no staying .

5   In despite of the devils and hell, have through the very*
    middest of you !

6   And heavens and honor be witness that
    no want of resolution in me, but only my followers
    base and ignominious treasons, makes me betake me to
    my heels.

Cade

1   Was ever Feather so lightly blowne too & fro,
     as this multitude ?

2   The name of Henry the fift, hales them
     to an hundred mischiefes, and makes them leave mee de-
     solate .

3   I see them lay their heades together to surprize
     me .

4   My sword make way for me, for heere is no staying :
     in despight of the divels and hell, have through the verie
     middest of you, and heavens and honor be witnesse, that
     no want of resolution in mee, but onely my Followers
     base and ignominious treasons, makes me betake mee to
     my heeles .

- the extra breaths from the two extra commas in F #1-2 might suggest Cade's astonishment at his men's desertion

- with 2 of the 3 capitals occurring in the first two sentences, the rest of the speech is almost completely emotional (1/10 in six lines of F #3-4)

- as he begins his escape, the one surround phrase ' . My sword make way for me, for heere is no staying : ' sets up a much longer sentence ending the speech than set in modern texts, which split it into three: the F text suggests far more determination and perhaps energy/difficulty in getting through the mob than the modern texts show

The Third Part of
Henry the Sixt

Messenger

The Noble Duke of Yorke {is} slaine,
2.1.46 - 67

Background: the only speech for the character; as such it is self-explanatory.

Style: direct address to three men, in front of a larger group

Where: in the open in Herefordshire

To Whom: Yorke's three sons, Edward, George, and Richard, in front of their forces

# of Lines: 20

Probable Timing: 1.00 minutes

Take Note: F's orthography and sentence structure present not only the message but also the humanity of the Messenger, for it seems s/he cannot stay completely unattached - as the speech develops, so his/her feelings start to flood the delivery of the facts.

Messenger

1 {†} {T}he noble Duke of York {is} slain,
　 Your princely father and my loving lord !

2 　 Environed he was with many foes,
　 And stood against them, as the hope of Troy
　 Against the Greeks that would have ent'red Troy .

3 　 But Hercules himself must yield to odds;
　 And many strokes, though with a little axe,
　 Hews down and fells the hardest-timber'd oak.

4 　 By many hands your father was subdu'd,
　 But only slaught'red by the ireful arm
　 Of unrelenting Clifford and the queen :
　 Who crown'd the gracious Duke in high despite,
　 Laugh'd in his face ; and when with grief he wept,
　 The ruthless Queen gave him to dry his cheeks
　 A napkin steeped in the harmless blood
　 Of sweet young Rutland, by rough Clifford slain .

5 　 And after many scorns, many foul taunts,
　 They took his head, and on the gates of York
　 They set the same, and there it doth remain,
　 The saddest spectacle that e'er I view'd .

Messenger

1 {†} {T}he Noble Duke of Yorke {is} slaine,
   Your Princely Father, and my loving Lord .

2   Environed he was with many foes,
   And stood against them, as the hope of Troy
   Against the Greekes, that would have entred Troy .

3   But Hercules himselfe must yeeld to oddes :
   And many stroakes, though with a little Axe,
   Hewes downe and fells the hardest-tymber'd Oake .

4   By many hands your Father was subdu'd,
   But onely slaught'red by the irefull Arme
   Of un-relenting Clifford, and the Queene :
   Who crown'd the gracious Duke in high despight,
   Laugh'd in his face : and when with griefe he wept,
   The ruthlesse Queene gave him, to dry his Cheekes,
   A Napkin, steeped in the harmelesse blood
   Of sweet young Rutland, by rough Clifford slaine :
   And after many scornes, many foule taunts,
   They tooke his Head, and on the Gates of Yorke
   They set the same, and there it doth remaine,
   The saddest spectacle that ere I view'd .

- the two surround phrases concisely sum up the message, both the highly emotional capture of the Duke of Yorke ' . But Hercules himselfe must yeeld oddes : ' and Margaret's utter contempt ' : Who crown'd the gracious Duke in high despight,/Laugh'd in his face : '

- at the start (F #1-2) s/he stays in full control (9/3 in five lines), but already the first of the five extra breath-thoughts is seen in line 2, suggesting the need for an extra breath for both clarity and self-control

- as the capture of the Duke is first mentioned, the Messenger's personal feelings swamp the previously seen intellect (F #3, 3/8 in three lines!)

- and as the Messenger expands on the capture of Yorke; on Margaret's offering him the blood of his youngest son; and of Yorke's beheading, the F speech ends in one onrushed 12 line passionate sentence (13/15 up until its last two lines), suggesting the loss of objectivity – a loss most modern texts spoil by splitting the sentence in two: while grammatically correct, modern texts' rewrite essentially supports just the reporting the details of Yorke's death (the first sentence mt. #4), and his beheading (mt. #5); F's onrush seems to highlight the effects of the event on the Messenger as well

The Third Part of
Henry the Sixt

Son/Sonne

Ill blowes the winde that profits no body,
2.5.55 - 72

Background: whether the following speeches are figments of Henry's tortured imagination or actual events, the pain of discovery for each character is palpable in the extreme. Both speeches are the only ones for each character, and as such they are self explanatory.

Style: each solo

Where: close to the battlefield in Yorkshire

To Whom: a dead body, self, and direct audience address

# of Lines: 18

Probable Timing: 0.55 minutes

Take Note: The extra commas ending the opening two F lines suggest an onrolling sentence probably supporting the physical activity of dragging the body of the man he has just killed. Similarly, F allows the tremendous shock of discovering it is his father that he has killed due weight by setting the two unusually short sentences #2-3. Modern texts seem to mute both events by splitting F1 in two, and setting F #3 as the start of a new sentence, mt. #4.

Son

1   Ill blows the wind that profits nobody.

2   This man whom hand to hand I slew in fight
     May be possessed with some store of crowns,
     And I that, haply, take them from him now,
     May yet, ere night, yield both my life and them
     To some man else, as this dead man doth me .

3   Who's this?

4   O God ! it is my father's face,
     Whom in this conflict I, unwares, have kill'd .

5   O heavy times ! begetting such events !

6   From London by the King was I press'd forth,
     My father, being the Earl of Warwick's man,
     Came on the part of York, press'd by his master ;
     And I, who at his hands receiv'd my life,
     Have by my hands, of life bereaved him .

7   Pardon me, God, I knew not what I did !
     And pardon father, for I knew not thee !

8   My tears shall wipe away these bloody marks;
     And no more words till they have flow'd their fill .

Sonne

1   Ill blowes the winde that profits no body,
This man whom hand to hand I slew in fight,
May be possessed with some store of Crownes,
And I that (haply) take them from him now,
May yet (ere night) yeeld both my Life and them
To some man else, as this dead man doth me .

2   Who's this?

3   Oh God !

4   It is my Fathers face,
Whom in this Conflict, I (unwares) have kill'd :
Oh heavy times ! begetting such Events .

5   From London, by the King was I prest forth,
My Father being the Earle of Warwickes man,
Came on the part of Yorke, prest by his Master :
And I, who at his hands receiv'd my life,
Have by my hands, of Life bereaved him .

6   Pardon me God, I knew not what I did :
And pardon Father, for I knew not thee .

7   My Teares shall wipe away these bloody markes :
And no more words, till they have flow'd their fill .

- from the moment of discovery, the speech can be summed up by the first surround phrase with its very rare exclamation mark
    " : Oh heavy times ! Begetting such Events . "
while the devastating effect on the Son is marked by the four successive surround phrases that end the speech
    " . Pardon me God, I knew not what I did:/ And pardon me Father, for I knew not thee . / My Teares shall wipe away these bloody markes : / And no more words, till they have flow'd their fill . "

- even after the emotional first line (0/2), the speech shows little intellectual energy, till the discovery of the identity of the dead man, perhaps suggesting that the battle had taken much out of the character (2/4 in six and a half lines, F #1-2)

- but once the discovery is made, surprisingly, intellect rather than passion freely flows (perhaps suggesting that the character is too stunned to fully emote (F #3-5, 12/5)

- the apology to God and his father is purely intellectual (2/0)

- and, while the opening of the final sentence is both intellectual and emotional (1/2), the last line is icy calm, as if finally everything is leached out of him

Father

Thou that so stoutly hath resisted me,
between 2.5.79 - 122

Background: The pain of discovery for each character is palpable in the extreme. Both speeches are the only ones for each character, and as such they are self explanatory.

Style: solo

Where: close to the battlefield in Yorkshire

To Whom: a dead body, self, and direct audience address

# of Lines: 26

Probable Timing: 1.15 minutes

Take Note: While the images of the pain of the situation are easily discernible in both texts, F offers some surprises, especially at the start and finish of the scene.

Father

1 Thou that so stoutly hath resisted me,
   Give me thy gold - if thou hast any gold -
   For I have bought it with an hundred blows.

2 But let me see : is this our foeman's face ?

3 Ah, no, no, no, it is mine only son !

4 Ah, boy, if any life be left in thee,
   Throw up thine eye !

5 See, see, what show'rs arise,
   Blown with the windy tempest of my heart
   Upon thy wounds, that kills mine eye and heart !

6 O, pity, God, this miserable age !

7 What stratagems ! how fell !how butcherly !
   Erroneous, mutinous, and unnatural,
   This deadly quarrel daily doth beget !

8 O boy ! thy father gave thee life too soon,
   And hath bereft thee of thy life too late.

   _____

9 How will my wife for slaughter of my son
   Shed seas of tears, and ne'er be satisfied !

   _____

10 These arms of mine shall be thy winding sheet ;
   My heart, sweet boy, shall be thy sepulchre,
   For from my heart thine image ne'er shall go ;
   My sighing breast shall be thy funeral bell ;
   And so obsequious will thy father be,
   [E'en] for the loss of thee, having no more,
   As Priam was for all his valiant sons.

11 I'll bear thee hence, and let them fight that will,
   For I have murthered where I should not kill.

Father

1   Thou that so stoutly hath resisted me,
    Give me thy Gold, if thou hast any Gold:
    For I have bought it with an hundred blowes.

2   But let me see: Is this our Foe-mans face?

3   Ah, no, no, no, it is mine onely Sonne.

4   Ah Boy, if any life be left in thee,
    Throw up thine eye: see, see, what showres arise,
    Blowne with the windie Tempest of my heart,
    Upon thy wounds, that killes mine Eye, and Heart.

5   O pitty God, this miserable Age!

6   What Stra{ta}gems? how fell? how Butcherly?
    Erreoneous, mutinous, and unnaturall,
    This deadly quarrell daily doth beget?

7   O Boy! thy Father gave thee life too soone,
    And hath bereft thee of thy life too late.

---

8   How will my Wife, for slaughter of my Sonne,
    Shed seas of Teares and ne're be satisfi'd?

---

9   These armes of mine shall be thy winding sheet:
    My heart (sweet Boy) shall be thy Sepulcher,
    For from my heart, thine Image ne're shall go.

10 My sighing brest, shall be thy Funerall bell;
    And so obsequious will thy Father be,
    [Men] for the losse of thee, having no more,
    As Priam was for all his Valiant Sonnes,
    Ile beare thee hence, and let them fight that will,
    For I have murthered where I should not kill.

- the preponderance of capitals in F's first two sentences (4/1) plus the surround phrases

    " : For I have bought it with an hundred blowes . / But let me see : Is this our Foe-mans face ? "

    could indicate an almost jaunty opening to the speech, with the second short F #2 suggesting an almost indecent hurry to see who he has killed

- then two more short sentences (F #3 and #5) strip the Father's life down to an unavoidable series of truths which, after the shock of discovering he has killed his son (1/2 in the one line F #3), seems intellectually unavoidable (8/4, for the next six lines, F #4 to the first line of #6)

- for a moment the battle that has brought them to this brings his feelings forth (0/3, the last two lines of F #6)

- and then, though he cannot completely switch off his mind, feelings continue to be voiced until the last line and a half of the speech (13/9)

- the ungrammatical setting of F #9-10 shows a far more disturbed man than the modern texts, for where

    a/ the F period separating the two comes at an emotional breakpoint, suggesting that he has to take a pause before continuing, via the surround phrase with the only (emotional) semicolon in the speech, " . My sighing brest, shall be thy Funerall bell ; " most modern texts refuse him the pause and reset the moment as an ongoing semicolon, and

    b/ while the act of taking his son offstage is treated in F as a grief-stricken inevitable outcome stemming directly from his lament (by connecting the thoughts via a fast-link comma), most modern texts set their new (grammatical) sentence here, thus creating a far more controlled and rational moment than was originally set

- but inescapable bleakness hits once more in the last non-embellished line and half, 'and let them fight that will, / For I have murthered where I should not kill.'

King {Henry}

O pitteous spectacle ! O bloody Times !
between 2.5.73 - 124

Background: the following is Henry's response to the prior speeches of Son and Father,

Style: solo

Where: close to the battlefield in Yorkshire

To Whom: self, and direct audience address

# of Lines: 19

Probable Timing: 1.00 minutes

Take Note: The large amount of major punctuation (7 colons and two semicolons, a very large number for such a short speech) suggest that Henry's brain is working overtime. Indeed, the long sentence F #4, split into six separate sentences in most modern texts, suggests that this is the first of what could be described as an overload/ brain-storm/breakdown.

King

1   O piteous spectacle!

2   O bloody times!

3   Whiles lions war and battle for their dens,
    Poor harmless lambs abide their enmity.

4   Weep, wretched man :   I'll aid thee tear for tear,
    And let our hearts and eyes, like civil war,
    Be blind with tears, and break o'ercharg'd with grief .

---

5   Woe above woe! grief, more [than] common grief !

6   O that my death would stay these ruthful deeds !

7   O, pity, pity, gentle heaven, pity!

8   The red rose and the white are on his face,
    The fatal colors of our striving houses ;
    The one his purple blood right well resembles,
    The other his pale cheeks, methinks, presenteth .

9   Wither one rose, and let the other flourish :
    If you contend, a thousand lives must wither.

10/ Was ever king so griev'd for subjects' woe?

11 Much is your sorrow ;   mine ten times so much.

---

12 Sad-hearted-men, much overgone with care,
    Here sits a King more woeful [than] you are.

King

1   O pitteous spectacle !

2   O bloody Times !

3   Whiles Lyons Warre, and battaile for their Dennes,
     Poore harmlesse Lambes abide their enmity .

4   Weepe wretched man : Ile ayde thee Teare for Teare,
     And let our hearts and eyes, like Civill Warre,
     Be blinde with teares, and break ore-charg'd with griefe

---

Wo above wo :greefe, more [thé] common greefe
O that my death would stay these ruthfull deeds :
O pitty, pitty, gentle heaven pitty :
The Red Rose and the White are on his face,
The fatall Colours of our striving Houses :
The one, his purple Blood right well resembles,
The other his pale Cheekes (me thinkes) presenteth :
Wither one Rose, and let the other flourish :
If you contend, a thousand lives must wither .

---

5   Was ever King so greev'd for Subjects woe?

6   Much is your sorrow ; Mine, ten times so much .

7   Sad-hearted-men, much overgone with Care ;
     Heere sits a King, more wofull [then] you are .

- the large number of surround phrases thus created are testament for the pain he feels he caused in others coming back to haunt him – the opening of F #4, the whole of F #7 and #8, plus those contained in the anguished onrush of F #5

  " : O pitty, pitty, gentle heaven pitty ; "

  and referring to the rose symbols of Yorke (white) and Lancaster (red)

  " : Wither one Rose, and let the other flourish ; /If you contend, a thousand lives must wither. "

- though his mind is working in the opening three F sentences and first three lines of F #4 (8 capitals in the six lines), his emotions are already swamping him, especially with the verbal weight of the long spellings (18 in all) emphasising the beginning or the end of a phrase or idea

- then, in F #4's next three lines, feelings take over completely (0/6)

- but, as he sees the symbol of the guilt of the two rival houses in the blood and death-mask of the dead son, so his intellect takes over for the rest of the speech (the remainder of F #4 through to #6, 11/5) by F #7, with the two unusually short sentences preceding it, and with the logical colons found in the middle of the speech now giving way to two (emotional) semicolons, it seems that Henry is finally sub-sumed by his woe, with the dry intellect of the penultimate line (1/0) and the final, emotional semicolon led, single line self-description (1/2)

Clifford

Heere burnes my Candle out ; I, heere it dies,

2.6.1 - 30

Background: unfortunately, Clifford's fine words advising Henry to 'steele thy melting heart, /To hold thine owne,' and fight to maintain the throne for his son instead of surrendering it to Yorke as promised has only led to his own death in the ensuing battle. The quarto stage direction simply reads 'Enter Clifford wounded, with an arrow in his necke'.

Style: solo

Where: the battlefield

To Whom: direct audience address

# of Lines: 29

Probable Timing: 1.30 minutes

Take Note: F's sentence structure clearly sets up a series of early political realisations for the dying Clifford, whereas the modern texts seem to restructure the sentences into a lament. Similarly, the two longer F sentences finishing the speech show the power of a dying man succeeding in keeping his thoughts ongoing: most modern texts split both sentences, the spurts thus created suggesting a man giving in to his fading energies.

Clifford

1   Here burns my candle out ; ay, here it dies,
    Which whiles it lasted, gave King Henry light .

2   O Lancaster !

3   I fear thy overthrow
    More [than] my body's parting with my soul .

4   My love and fear glu'd many friends to thee,
    And now I fall, thy tough commixtures melts,
    Impairing Henry, strength'ning misproud York ;
    [The common people swarm like summer flies,]
    And whether fly the gnats but to the sun?

5   And who shines now, but Henry's enemies?

6   O Phoebus ! hadst thou never given consent
    That Phaeton should check thy fiery steeds,
    Thy burning car never had scorch'd the earth .

7   And, Henry, hadst thou sway'd as kings should do,
    Or as thy father, and his father did,
    Giving no ground unto the house of York,
    They never then had sprung like summer flies;
    I and ten thousand in this luckless realm
    {Had } left no mourning widows for our death,
    And thou this day hadst kept thy chair in peace .

8   For what doth cherish weeds but gentle air?
    And what makes robbers bold but too much lenity?

9   Bootless are plaints, and cureless are my wounds ;
    No way to fly, nor strength to hold [our] flight .

10 The foe is merciless, and will not pity;
    For at their hands I have deserved no pity .

11 The air hath got into my deadly wounds,
    And much effuse of blood doth make me faint .

12 Come, York and Richard, Warwick and the rest,
    I stabb'd your fathers' bosoms, split my brest .

Clifford

1　Heere burnes my Candle out ; I, heere it dies,
　 Which whiles it lasted, gave King Henry light .

2　O Lancaster !

3　　　　　　　　　I feare thy overthrow,
　 More [then] my Bodies parting with my Soule :
　 My Love and Feare, glew'd many Friends to thee,
　 And now I fall .

4　　　　　　　　Thy tough Commixtures melts,
　 Impairing Henry, strength'ning misproud Yorke ;

　　　　　　　　　　　∞
　 And whether flye the Gnats, but to the Sunne?

5　And who shines now, but Henries Enemies?

6　O Phoebus ! had'st thou never given consent,
　 That Phaeton should checke thy fiery Steeds,
　 Thy burning Carre never had scorch'd the earth .

7　And Henry, had'st thou sway'd as Kings should do,
　 Or as thy Father, and his Father did,
　 Giving no ground unto the house of Yorke,
　 They never then had sprung like Sommer Flyes :
　 I, and ten thousand in this lucklesse Realme,
　 {Had} left no mourning Widdowes for our death,
　 And thou this day, had'st kept thy Chaire in peace .

8　For what doth cherrish Weeds, but gentle ayre?
　 And what makes Robbers bold, but too much lenity?

9　Bootlesse are Plaints, and Curelesse are my Wounds :
　 No way to flye, nor strength to hold [out] flight :
　 The Foe is mercilesse, and will not pitty :
　 For at their hands I have deserved no pitty .

10　The ayre hath got into my deadly Wounds,
　 And much effuse of blood, doth make me faint :
　 Come Yorke, and Richard, Warwicke, and the rest,
　 I stab'd your Fathers bosomes ; Split my brest .

- F's unusually short sentences #2 and #5 show that Clifford's thoughts are fixed on the plight of the king rather than on his own death

- the four surround phrases comprising all of F #9 show why, starting with the passionate (3/2 in one line) ' . Bootlesse are Plaints, and Cureless are my Wounds : " and ending with the bleak " : For at their hands I have deserved no pitty . "

- there are only three (emotional) semicolons in the speech, all of which intensify other surround phrases - the fear that in losing the current battle Henry will be abandoned by his weak allies (' ; And whether flye the Gnats, but to the Sunne . '), plus two comments on his own inevitable death - the opening (' . Heere burnes my Candle out ; ') and the final appeal for (a soldier's?) death from his enemies (' ; Split my breast . ')

- passion is the hallmark of the opening three F sentences, with intellect slightly more prevalent than emotion as Clifford realises that with his death his own allies might well leave Henry (9/6)

- then his mind seems to focus more clearly as he elaborates this potential loss even further in the next three F sentences (#4-6 12/5), and this mental overdrive continues into the first four lines of F #7 as he realises that all of this has come about through Henry's ignoble betrayal in handing over the crown (7/2)

- then passion breaks through until almost the end of the speech as Clifford realises the hopelessness of both the political situation and its fall-out on everyone's personal life, especially his own (9/12 in the nine lines mid F #7 to F #9)

- F's last sentence neatly sums up his dying energies: in the first realisation of what is happening to him, both mind and emotion are at work (1/1); then comes one line of calm as if he were saving his energy for the final two-line, courageously defiant, death-call to his enemies 5/3)

King Henry

M. Lieutenant, now that God and Friends
between 4.6.1 –25

Background: in the continually fluctuating and topsy-turvey world of 'now the Lancastrian Henry is King, and now the Yorkist Edward is', Henry has been rescued from an apparently comfortable imprisonment in the Tower of London and once more reinstated as King. Here is his response to his ex-jailer, the Lieutenant of the Tower, who has just prayed for 'pardon of your Majestie'.

Style: one on one address in front of a larger group

Where: the Tower of London

To Whom: the Lieutenant, in front of his rescuers Somerset, Oxford, Henry Richmond, Warwicke and his brother Montague, and, temporarily on the Lancastrian side, the Yorkist middle brother, George

# of Lines: 21 Probable Timing: 1.10 minutes

Take Note: For a release-from-imprisonment speech, there is a great deal of to-ing and fro-ing in style, suggesting that Henry may be much more disturbed than the words themselves suggest.

King Henry

1   [Master] Lieutenant, now that God and friends
    Have shaken Edward from the regal seat,
    And turn'd my captive state to liberty,
    My fear to hope, my sorrows unto joys,
    At our enlargement what are thy due fees?

---

2   Nay, be thou sure, I'll well requite thy kindness,
    For that it made my imprisonment a pleasure ;
    [Ay], such a pleasure, as incaged birds
    Conceive, when, after many moody thoughts,
    At last, by notes of household harmony
    They quite forget their loss of liberty .

3   But, Warwick, after God, thou set'st me free,
    And chiefly therefore I thank God, and thee .

4   He was the author, thou the instrument .

5   Therefore that I may conquer fortune's spite
    By living low, where fortune cannot hurt me,
    And that the people of this blessed land
    May not be punish'd with my thwarting stars,
    Warwick, although my head still wear the crown,
    I here resign my government to thee,
    For thou art fortunate in all thy deeds .

King Henry

1　　[M.] Lieutenant, now that God and Friends
　　　Have shaken Edward from the Regall seate,
　　　And turn'd my captive state to libertie,
　　　My feare to hope, my sorrowes unto joyes,
　　　At our enlargement what are thy due Fees?

2　　Nay, be thou sure, Ile well requite thy kindnesse .

3　　For that it made my imprisonment, a pleasure :
　　　[I], such a pleasure, as incaged Birds
　　　Conceive ; when after many moody Thoughts,
　　　At last, by Notes of Houshold harmonie,
　　　They quite forget their losse of Libertie .

4　　But Warwicke, after God, thou set'st me free,
　　　And chiefely therefore, I thanke God, and thee,
　　　He was the Author, thou the Instrument .

5　　Therefore that I may conquer Fortunes spight,
　　　By living low, where Fortune cannot hurt me,
　　　And that the people of this blessed Land
　　　May not be punisht with my thwarting starres,
　　　Warwicke, although my Head still weare the Crowne,
　　　I here resigne my Government to thee,
　　　For thou art fortunate in all thy deeds .

- the surround phrases ' . For that it made my imprisonment, a plea-sure : /I, such a pleasure, as incaged Birds/Conceive ; ' with its accom-panying (emotional) semicolon, the only one in the speech, set up the possible root of the disturbance - perhaps the 'saint'-like Henry does not wish to be released back to the outside world

- this would explain the wished for handing over the crown to Warwicke (F #5) which opens intellectually and finishes more emo-tionally (3/0 in the first three lines, 3/5 in the last four)

- the 'thanking God and Warwicke' slightly onrushed F #4 (split into two by modern texts) is also a sign of less than grammatical nice-ties, with what modern texts set as their separate sentence #4 being fast-linked in F by a comma, the whole again reinforcing the idea of Henry's passionate religious zeal (5/3 in just three lines)

- the F #1 opening thanks to his one-time jailor shows lack of consis-tency: it opens with strong intellectual strength (5/2 in the first two lines); followed by a line of foreshortened non-embellishment ('liber-tie'); followed by a single highly emotional line 'My feare to hope, my sorrowes unto joyes,' (suggesting just how raw an emotional state he may be in)

- the act of thanks (F #2-3) is deemed ungrammatical by most modern texts, for the short single line F #2, (where F's perhaps ungrammati-cal period suggests that Henry needs a substantial pause before con-tinuing), is not set by most modern texts, which join the two sentenc-es together

{King} Henry

So flies the wreaklesse shepherd from Wolfe :
between 5.6.7 - 56

Background: following his part in the killing of Henry's son, the
youngest Yorkist brother Richard is about to embark on one of the
final acts of the civil war, the cold-blooded killing of King Henry,
once more imprisoned in the Tower of London. The following is
triggered by Richard's dismissal of the Lieutenant, leaving him
alone with Henry.

Style: as part of a two-handed scene

Where: the Tower of London

To Whom: the Yorkist Richard

# of Lines: 28

Probable Timing: 1.25 minutes

Take Note: Faced with death, Henry shows not only the expected passion as he denounces Richard, but also some unexpected calm.

Henry

1   So flies the [reckless] shepherd from [the] wolf;
     So first the harmless sheep doth yield his fleece,
     And next his throat unto the butcher's knife .

2   What scene of death hath [Roscius] now to act?

_____

3 {†} Wherefore dost thou come?

4   Is't for my life?

_____

5 {†} {My} son {thou} kill'd for his presumption .

6   Hadst thou been kill'd, when first [thou] didst presume,
     Thou had'st not liv'd to kill a son of mine .

7   And thus I prophesy, that many a thousand
     Which now mistrust no parcel of my fear,
     And many an old man's sigh, and many a widow's,
     And many an orphan's water-standing-eye -
     Men for their sons, wives for their husbands,
     Orphans for their parents timeless death -
     Shall rue the hour that ever thou was't born .

8   The owl shriek'd at thy birth, an evil sign;
     The night-crow cried, aboding luckless time ;
     Dogs howl'd, and hideous [tempests] shook down trees;
     The raven rook'd her on the chimney's top,
     And chatt'ring pies in dismal discords sung ;
     Thy mother felt more [than] a mother's pain,
     And yet brought forth less [than] a mother's hope,
     To wit, an [indigest] and deformed lump,
     Not like the fruit of such a goodly tree .

9   Teeth had'st thou in thy head when thou was't born,
     To signify thou cam'st to bite the world ;
     And if the rest be true which I have heard,
     Thou cam'st _____

Henry

1   So flies the [wreaklesse] shepherd from [] Wolfe :
    So first the harmlesse Sheepe doth yeeld his Fleece,
    And next his Throate, unto the Butchers Knife .

2   What Scene of death hath [Rossius] now to Acte?

___

3 {†} Wherefore dost thou come?

4   Is't for my Life?

___

5 {†} {My} Son {thou} kill'd for his presumption .

6   Hadst thou bin kill'd, when first [ÿ] didst presume,
    Thou had'st not liv'd to kill a Sonne of mine :
    And thus I prophesie, that many a thousand,
    Which now mistrust no parcell of my feare,
    And many an old mans sighe, and many a Widdowes,
    And many an Orphans water-standing-eye,
    Men for their Sonnes, Wives for their Husbands,
    Orphans, for their Parents timeles death,
    Shall rue the houre that ever thou was't borne .

7   The Owle shriek'd at thy birth, an evill signe,
    The Night-Crow cry'de, aboding lucklesse time,
    Dogs howl'd, and hiddeous [Tempest] shook down Trees:
    The Raven rook'd her on the Chimnies top,
    And chatt'ring Pies in dismall Discords sung :
    Thy Mother felt more [then] a Mothers paine,
    And yet brought forth lesse [then] a Mothers hope,
    To wit, an [indigested] and deformed lumpe,
    Not like the fruit of such a goodly Tree .

8   Teeth had'st thou in thy head, when thou was't borne,
    To signifie, thou cam'st to bite the world :
    And if the rest be true, which I have heard,
    Thou cam'st _____

- in F #1's all-condemning, all-summarizing sentence – including the wonderfully wry opening surround phrase summarising the jailer's desertion of him - Henry's passion is given full rein (6/6 in three lines)

- but then, in the three unusually short sentences (F #2-4) as Henry challenges the man who killed his son as to whether he is about to kill him too, a calm mental control rises to the fore (4/1 in two lines)

- however, by F #6, finally able to speak his mind, his passion returns - but only after an icy-calm of lines 1 and 3 (dealing with the wished for early-death-as-child for Richard, and the start of his act of prophecy)

- then his outspoken release starts to grow (6/8 in the last six lines) as he moves from his son's death to the misery Richard has brought to the world at large – unfortunately, the impact of the onrush of F's sentence #6 is gutted by being split in two by most modern texts)

- then, as Henry centres his attack directly on Richard (F #7), the passion hits full stride (13/10 in nine lines)

- but for whatever reason (exhaustion? realising the futility of it all?), F #8 displays a totally different speaking pattern
  a/ there is just one long spelling, in the first line
  b/ followed by two-and a-half non-embellished lines
  c/ the whole (monosyllabic save for one choked-back word, the short-spelled 'signifie') broken up by three extra breath-thoughts

perhaps suggesting that Henry is so overwhelmed by the energies and thoughts he has released to date, that he needs the extra breaths to be able to control/centre himself in order to continue his prophecy-turned-harangue

2. Murtherer

Ile not meddle with {conscience}, . . .

1.4.134 - 144

Background: though hired by Richard to kill brother Clarence, the 2nd Murtherer initially expressed doubts. These quickly vanished when his colleague reminded him of the money Richard will pay for a job well done, so much so that now the 2nd Murtherer dismisses conscience for the interference in his life it has already caused.

Style: as part of a two handed scene

Where: the Tower of London

To Whom: the 1st Murtherer

# of Lines: 10

Probable Timing: 0.35 minutes

Take Note: F's onrush throughout suggests an urgency in release (indignant? a passionate response to previous harm his conscience has done?): most modern texts gut the onrush by splitting all three F sentences (F #1 = mt. #1-2; F #2 = mt. #3-4; F #3 = mt. #5-7).

2. Murtherer

1   I'll not meddle with {conscience}, it makes a man a coward .

2   A man cannot steal, but it accuseth him ;a man cannot
swear, but it checks him ;a man cannot lie with his
neighbor's wife, but it detects him .

3   'Tis a blushing
shamefac'd spirit that mutinies in a man's bosom .

4   It
fills a man full of obstacles .

5   It made me once restore a
purse of gold that (by chance) I found .

6   It beggars any
man that keeps it .

7   It is turn'd out of towns and cit-
ties for a dangerous thing, and every man that means to
live well endeavors to trust to himself , and live without it .

2. Murtherer

1 Ile not meddle with {conscience}, it makes a man a Coward :
A man cannot steale, but it accuseth him : A man cannot
Sweare, but it Checkes him : A man cannot lye with his
Neighbours Wife, but it detects him .

2   'Tis a blushing
shamefac'd spirit, that mutinies in a mans bosome : It
filles a man full of Obstacles .

3   It made me once restore a
Pursse of Gold that (by chance) I found : It beggars any
man that keepes it : It is turn'd out of Townes and Cit-
ties for a dangerous thing, and every man that means to
live well, endevours to trust to himselfe, and live without it .

- the 6 colons in just 10 lines suggest he is trying to be logical
- that all but the last half of F #3 is composed of 8 surround phrases suggests his diatribe against conscience is very important
- both F #1 and #2 are essentially passionate (6/5 in three and a half lines and 2/2 in two lines respectively)
- it's only by F #3 that any form of mental control is established (6/3 in the four lines up to the last comma)
- while the idea of doing without 'it' (conscience) expressed in the last phrase of the speech, is non-embellished, the build up to 'it' is momentarily emotional (0/2 in the penultimate phrase)

3. Citizen

Neighbours, God speed .
between 2.3.6 - 45

Background: following the death of King Edward, citizens gather to discuss what may quickly become a very bleak future. As an expression of two sets of fears, a country being ruled by a child, and the political dangers that might stem from Richard (his formal title is the 'Duke of Glouster', as mentioned in the third sentence) ,the speech is self-explanatory.

Style: part of a three-handed scene, perhaps in front of a larger group

Where: unspecified, but probably a street in London

To Whom: fellow Citizens of London, two of whom are given lines

# of Lines: 15

Probable Timing: 0.50 minutes

3. Citizen

1   Neighbors, God speed ! {†}

2   {If} the news hold{s} of good king Edward's death, {†}
     Then master's look to see a troublous world .

3   Woe to that land that's govern'd by a child! {†} }

---

4 {†} Who shall now be nearest
       Will touch us all too near, if God prevent not {.}

5 {†} Full of danger is the Duke of [Gloucester] {.}

---

6   When clouds are seen, wise men put on their cloaks;
     When great leaves fall, then winter is at hand ;
     When the sun sets, who doth not look for night ?

7   Untimely storms makes men expect a dearth .

8   All may be well ; but if God sort it so,
     'Tis more [than] we deserve or I expect .

---

9 {†} The water swell before a boist'rous storm.

10   But leave it all to God .

3. Citizen

1   Neighbours, God speed . {†}

2   {If} the newes hold{s} of good king Edwards death, {†}
     Then Masters looke to see a troublous world .

3   Woe to that Land that's govern'd by a Childe . {†}

---

4 {†} Who shall now be neerest,
     Will touch us all too neere, if God prevent not {.}

5 {†} Full of danger is the Duke of [Glouster] {.}

---

6   When Clouds are seen, wisemen put on their clokes ;
     When great leaves fall, then Winter is at hand ;
     When the Sun sets, who doth not looke for night ?

7   Untimely stormes, makes men expect a Dearth :
     All may be well ; but if God sort it so,
     'Tis more [then] we deserve, or I expect .

---

8 {†} The Water swell before a boyst'rous storme :
     But leave it all to God .

- that three of the eight F sentences are short suggests that the Citizen is addressing something of great importance for all of them

- that the five pieces of major punctuation are only found in the latter half of the speech (F #6-8) as the dangers of Richard are hinted at, and that three of them are semicolons, gives added testimony to the intellectual and emotional struggle the Citizen is undergoing

- and if this weren't enough, the fact that all three concluding sentences are composed of surround phrases adds even more to the impact of what the Citizen is feeling and arguing

- the speech starts off in passion (F #1-4, 6/6)

- but the single line sentence broaching the danger Richard represents is clearly intellectual (2/0, F #5)

- the (surround phrase) nature image analogy is also (carefully?) mentally controlled (F #6-7, 5/2)

- while the final summary and suggestion of leaving all to God (F #8) falls back to passion once again (2/2)

Scrivener

Here is the Indictment of the good Lord Hastings,
3.6.1 - 14

Background: this is the only speech for this character, who has prepared a legal manuscript of formal indictment specifying the
charges being brought against Hastings, one of Richard's many vic-
tims. However, as the Scrivener explains, the timing doesn't seem
quite right.

Style: solo

Where: unspecified

To Whom: direct audience address

# of Lines: 14

Probable Timing: 0.45 minutes

Scrivener

1   Here is the indictment of the good Lord Hastings,
    Which in a set hand fairly is engross'd
    That it may be to-day read o'er in Paul's.

2   And mark how well the sequel hangs together :
    Eleven hours I have spent to write it over,
    For yesternight by Catesby was it sent me ;
    The precedent was full as long a doing,
    And yet within these five hours Hastings liv'd,
    Untainted, unexamin'd, free, at liberty .

3   Here's a good world the while !

4   Who is so gross
    That cannot see this palpable device ?

5   Yet [who's] so bold, but says he sees it not ?

6   Bad is the world, and all will come to [naught],
    When such ill dealing must be seen in thought .

Scrivener

1   Here is the Indictment of the good Lord Hastings,
Which in a set Hand fairely is engross'd,
That it may be to day read o're in Paules .

2   And marke how well the sequell hangs together :
Eleven houres I have spent to write it over,
For yester-night by Catesby was it sent me,
The Precedent was full as long a doing,
And yet within these five houres Hastings liv'd,
Untainted, unexamin'd, free, at libertie .

3   Here's a good World the while .

4   Who is so grosse, that cannot see this palpable device ?

5   Yet [who] so bold, but sayes he sees it not ?

6   Bad is the World, and all will come to [nought],
When such ill dealing must be seene in thought .

- the troubling point is beautifully singled out by the only non-embellished line in the speech 'Untainted, unexamin'd, free, at libertie.'

- that this disturbs the Scrivener can be seen in F's short sentences #3-4

- this is magnified by the fact that F sets both as irregular lines (6 syllables for F #3, 14 for F #4): it seems the Scrivener needs to pause after the enormous implied criticism inherent in F #3, and then blurts out the dilemma that faces him if he would dare to speak his mind (F #4): by regularising both lines to ten syllables, most modern texts have essentially wiped out the moment of crisis set by F

- while the speech starts with fairly controlled mental discipline (F #1, 5/2), the voicing of concern, marked by the surround phrase opening F #2, becomes emotional (0/3 in the first two lines)

- mental composure is then restored for the four remaining lines of F #2 and the single line F #3 (4/1), but, again, at the moment of expressed concern (F #4-5) emotion creeps back in (0/2)

- while the summary, F #6, still struggles between intellect (the first line) and emotion (the second)

Buckingham

Ah ha, my Lord, this Prince is not an Edward,
3.7.71 – 80 & 92 -5

Background: though failing to have the Mayor and Citizens acclaim Richard as King, Buckingham has persuaded them to accompany him to meet Richard at Baynard's Castle. In a stunning piece of manipulation Richard is about to appear accompanied by two priests and, apparently too pious to think of worldly matters, has sent the message via Catesby that they all return tomorrow since 'He is within, with two right reverend Fathers,/Divinely bent to Meditation/And in no Worldly suites would he be mov'd,/To draw him from his holy Exercise'. This gives Buckingham the perfect opening to soften up the Mayor and Citizens with the following.

Style: one on one for the benefit of a larger group

Where: a hall in Baynard's Castle

To Whom: the Mayor and Citizens of London

# of Lines: 13

Probable Timing: 0.45 minutes

Take Note: F's orthography shows an oratorically rhetorical master at his very best, for Buckingham's fast paced persuasion of the Mayor as to Richard's worth rapidly switches from intellect to passion to reinforce each point as he senses which approach will work best for which topic.

Buckingham

1   Ah ha, my lord, this prince is not an Edward !

2   He is not [lolling] on a lewd love-bed,
    But on his knees at meditation ;
    Not dallying with a brace of courtezans,
    But meditating with two deep divines ;
    Not sleeping, to engross his idle body,
    But praying, to enrich his watchful soul .

3   Happy were England, would this virtuous prince
    Take on his Grace the sovereignty thereof,
    But sure I fear we shall not win him to it .

---

4   When holy and devout religious men
    Are at their beads, 'tis much to draw them thence,
    So sweet is zealous contemplation .

Buckingham

1　Ah ha, my Lord, this Prince is not an Edward,
　He is not [lulling] on a lewd Love-Bed,
　But on his Knees, at Meditation :
　Not dallying with a Brace of Curtizans,
　But meditating with two deepe Divines :
　Not sleeping, to engrosse his idle Body,
　But praying, to enrich his watchfull Soule .

2　Happie were England, would this vertuous Prince
　Take on his Grace the Soveraigntie thereof .

3　But sure I feare we shall not winne him to it .

4　When holy and devout Religious men
　Are at their Beades, 'tis much to draw them thence,
　So sweet is zealous Contemplation .

- F #1's supposedly ungrammatical fast-link of the first line to the rest of the sentence testifies to the speed at which Buckingham is working on the Mayor: most modern texts remove this clue by setting the first line as a separate sentence

- Buckingham is at his intellectual best in the opening disparagement of Edward (9/0 in the first four lines of F#1), and then shifts to a passionate observation of Richard's obvious (!) religious depth (3/4 in F1's final three lines)

- Buckingham then reverts to intellect as he expresses the wish for Richard to become King (F #2, 4/0), only to go emotional in the rare short sentence expressing doubts that Richard will take it (F #3, 0/2), the explanation why (the final F #4) reverting to intellect once again (3/1)

Tyrrel

The tyrannous and bloodie Act is done,
4.3.1 - 22

Background: Tyrrel has been hired by Richard to bring about the death of his nephews, rightful heirs to the throne. The two children (Edward, rightfully the King, and his younger brother Richard) are now dead, having been smothered by Dighton and Forrest, the men Tyrrel employed to 'do this peece of ruthfull Butchery'. In the following ,Tyrrel describes the deaths of the Princes in the Tower, and the effect those deaths have had on all three adults involved.

Style: solo

Where: somewhere in the palace

To Whom: direct audience address

# of Lines: 24

Probable Timing: 1.15 minutes

Take Note: F's orthography suggests the speech falls into three parts with a coda.

Tyrrel

1　The tyrannous and bloody act is done,
　The most arch deed of piteous massacre
　That ever yet this land was guilty of.

2　Dighton and Forrest, who I did suborn
　To do this piece of [ruthless] butchery,
　Albeit they were flesh'd villains, bloody dogs,
　Melted with tenderness and [kind] compassion,
　Wept like [two] children in their deaths' sad story.

3　"O, thus," quoth Dighton, "lay the gentle babes."

4　"Thus, thus" (quoth Forrest) "girdling one another
　Within their alablaster innocent arms.

5　Their lips were four red roses on a stalk,
　[Which] in their summer beauty kiss'd each other.

6　A book of prayers on their pillow lay,
　Which [once]," quoth Forrest, "almost chang'd my mind;
　But O! the devil", there the villain stopp'd:
　When Dighton thus told on, "We smothered
　The most replenished sweet work of Nature
　That from the prime creation e'er she framed."

7　Hence both are gone with conscience and remorse
　They could not speak; and so I left them both,
　To bear this tidings to the bloody King.

Enter Richard

8　And here he comes.

9　　　　　　　　　All health my sovereign lord.

Tyrrel

1 The tyrannous and bloodie Act is done,
   The most arch deed of pittious massacre
   That ever yet this Land was guilty of:
   Dighton and Forrest, who I did suborne
   To do this peece of [ruthfull] Butchery,
   Albeit they were flesht Villaines, bloody Dogges,
   Melted with tendernesse, and [milde] compassion,
   Wept like [to] Children, in their deaths sad Story.

2 O thus (quoth Dighton) lay the gentle Babes:
   Thus, thus (quoth Forrest) girdling one another
   Within their Alablaster innocent Armes:
   Their lips were foure red Roses on a stalke,
   [And] in their Summer Beauty kist each other.

3 A Booke of Prayers on their pillow lay,
   Which[one] (quoth Forrest) almost chang'd my minde:
   But oh the Divell, there the Villaine stopt:
   When Dighton thus told on, we smothered
   The most replenished sweet worke of Nature,
   That from the prime Creation ere she framed.

4 Hence both are gone with Conscience and Remorse,
   They could not speake, and so I left them both,
   To beare this tydings to the bloody King.

Enter Richard

5 And heere he comes.

6   All health my Soveraigne Lord.

- the long F #1 describes both the act and the initial response of the two murderers he hired to do the deed: not surprisingly the sentence is passionate (9/6), and onrushed, as if Tyrrel is disturbed by what has occurred: most modern texts remove this disturbance by splitting F #1 in two

- F's onrush continues in #2, this time more intellectually than emotionally (11/5, including the first two lines of F #3), as he describes the two would-be murderers report of finding not just the beautiful children sleeping, but a prayer book protecting them as well: once more the onrush of F #2 is reduced by most modern texts, that this time split the sentence in three

- the third part of the speech (the last four lines of F #3 and all of F #4) reverts to passion (8/7) as Tyrrel deals with the eventual act of smothering the two princes to death and the fact the two men have not stayed, presumably for their reward

- as Richard arrives Tyrrel's pattern changes completely: all of a sudden he slips into two unusually short sentences, suggesting a great deal of care (and perhaps awkwardness?) especially since he has been left alone to make the final report to Richard (and with the overworked 2/1 of the final phrase, it may be that Tyrrel is exploiting the status game as far as may be dared)

The Tragedy of
Richard the Third

Buckingham

This is All-soules day (Fellow) is it not ?
between 5.1.10 - 29

Background: the one time right-hand of Richard, main confident and fully involved conspirator whose back-room machinations enabled Richard to achieve the crown, finally drew the line and would not help Richard murder his nephews in the Tower. Instead, Buckingham joined the ever-increasing numbers fighting against Richard and was captured. The following is his his last speech before execution.

Style: part of a two-handed scene in front of a small group

Where: unspecified, but presumably somewhere near Salisbury

To Whom: either a 'Sherife' (First Folio) or Ratcliffe (quartos), in front of guards

# of Lines: 19

Probable Timing: 1.00 minutes

Buckingham

1　This is All-Souls' day, fellow, is it not ?

2　Why then All-Souls' day is my body's doomsday .

3　This is the day which, in King Edward's time ,
　I wish'd might fall on me, when I was found
　False to his children and his wive's allies ;
　This is the day wherein I wish'd to fall
　By the false faith of him whom most I trusted ;
　This, this All-Souls' day to my fearful soul,
　Is the determin'd respite of my wrongs .

4　That high All-Seer, which I dallied with,
　Hath turn'd my feigned prayer on my head,
　And given in earnest what I begg'd in jest .

5　Thus doth he force the swords of wicked men
　To turn their own points in their masters' bosoms;
　Thus Margaret's curse falls heavy on my neck:
　"When he," quoth she, "shall split thy heart with sorrow,
　Remember Margaret was a Prophetess."

6　Come lead me, officers, to the block of shame ;
　Wrong hath but wrong, and blame the due of blame .

Buckingham

1   This is All-soules day (Fellow) is it not ?

---

2   Why then Al-soules day, is my bodies doomsday
    This is the day, which in King Edwards time
    I wish'd might fall on me, when I was found
    False to his Children, and his Wives Allies .

3   This is the day, wherein I wisht to fall
    By the false Faith of him whom most I trusted .

4   This, this All-soules day to my fearfull Soule,
    Is the determin'd respit of my wrongs :
    That high All-seer, which I dallied with,
    Hath turn'd my fained Prayer on my head,
    And given in earnest, what I begg'd in jest .

5   Thus doth he force the swords of wicked men
    To turne their owne points in their Masters bosomes .

6   Thus Margarets curse falles heavy on my necke :
    When he (quoth she) shall split thy heart with sorrow,
    Remember Margaret was a Prophetesse :
    Come leade me Officers to the blocke of shame,
    Wrong hath but wrong, and blame the due of blame .

- it seems likely that the only surround phrase in the speech, ' . Thus Margarets curse falles heavy on my necke : ' disturbs Buckingham's apparent equilibrium, especially since it starts a new F sentence #6 whereas it is folded into the larger mt. #5 by most modern texts

- also, while the strong intellectualism of the opening nine lines (12/5) suggests that Buckingham is fully in control of himself as he faces execution, yet with

  a/ F #1 being an unusually short sentence

  b/ the extra four breath-thoughts in F #2-3, perhaps suggesting that Buckingham needs extra breaths and pauses to control himself

  c/ and the fast-link connection of the first line of F #2, regarded as non-grammatical by most modern texts that start a new sentence (mt. #3) here,

  the strain underneath the mental discipline is very easy to see

- equally fascinating, in voicing his belief that he is about to get his just deserts, so, save for two capitalized words with religious connotations ('All-seer' and 'Prayer'), the next five lines (the last four lines of F #4 and the first line of F #5) are essentially non-embellished - as if the conclusion was inescapable

- fascinatingly, this non-embellished statement about punishment is repeated in the very last line of the speech (though this time he clearly states that he is being punished by someone equally blameworthy)

- whether this is a real or enforced calm depends how the previous five passionate lines (5/8, the last line of F #5 and the first four of F #6) are judged

The Life and Death of King John

Chatillion

Then turn your forces from this paltry siege,
2.1.54 - 78

Background: the French ambassador warns Philip of the imminent arrival of the English forces, as such the speech is self-explanatory. One note; the 'paltry siege' refers to the current plan to attack Angiers.

Style: one on one address for the benefit of the larger group

Where: outside Angiers

To Whom: King Philip, in front of his son Lewis the Dolphin, and French forces; the Duke of Austria; Constance and Arthur

# of Lines: 25

Probable Timing: 1.15 minutes

Take Note: Most unusually for a Herald, F sets the whole speech as one long sentence (as opposed to the modern texts splitting it into 7), which would suggest the niceties of normal reporting are being ignored because of the urgency of the situation. (It is suggested that readers work through the modern text sentence structure to understand each of the grammatical points being made before exploring F's onrush.)

Chatillion

1   Then turn your forces from this paltry siege,
    And stir them up against a mightier task .

2   England, impatient of your just demands,
    Hath put himself in arms.

3   The adverse winds
    Whose leisure I have stay'd, have given him time
    To land his legions all as soon as I ;
    His marches are expedient to this town,
    His forces strong, his soldiers confident .

4   With him along is come the mother- queen
    An [Ate]stirring him to blood and strife ;
    With her her niece, the Lady Blanch of Spain;
    With them a bastard of the king's deceas'd,
    And all th'unsettled humors of the land,
    Rash, inconsiderate, fiery voluntaries,
    With ladies' faces and fierce dragons' spleens,
    Have sold their fortunes at their native homes,
    Bearing their birthrights proudly on their backs,
    To make a hazard of new fortunes here .

5   In brief , a braver choice of dauntless spirits
    [Than] now the English bottoms have waft o'er
    Did never float upon the swelling tide,
    To do offense and scathe in Christendom .

                    [Drum beats]

6   The interruption of their churlish drums
    Cuts off more circumstance .

7   They are at hand,
    To parley or to fight, therefore prepare .

Chatillion

1   Then turne your forces from this paltry siege,
    And stirre them up against a mightier taske :
    England impatient of your just demands,
    Hath put himselfe in Armes, the adverse windes
    Whose leisure I have staid, have given him time
    To land his Legions all as soone as I :
    His marches are expedient to this towne,
    His forces strong, his Souldiers confident :
    With him along is come the Mother Queene,
    An [Ace] stirring him to bloud and strife,
    With her her Neece, the Lady Blanch of Spaine,
    With them a Bastard of the Kings deceast,
    And all th'unsetled humors of the Land,
    Rash, inconsiderate, fiery voluntaries,
    With Ladies faces, and fierce Dragons spleenes,
    Have sold their fortunes at their native homes,
    Bearing their birth-rights proudly on their backs,
    To make a hazard of new fortunes heere :
    In briefe, a braver choyse of dauntlesse spirits
    [Then] now the English bottomes have waft o're,
    Did never flote upon the swelling tide,
    To doe offence and scathe in Christendome :
    The interruption of their churlish drums
    Cuts off more circumstance, they are at hand,
                    [**Drum beats**]
    To parlie or to fight, therefore prepare .

- the opening two line announcement that a 'mightier taske' than Angiers faces them is emotional (0/3), and the four line explanation that John and his forces arrived at the same time as he did continues the emotion (2/4)

- the nine line detailed descriptions of the military strength and leaders accompanying John moves back towards the factual though it is still accompanied by his own feelings (13/8)

- surprisingly, Chatillion's two-line description of the English determination, starting with 'Have sold their fortunes . . .' is completely unembellished, and perhaps testament to just how strong the English force is, for . . .

- . . . the next three lines of summation, starting 'In briefe . . .', becomes very emotional for the first time since the two lines opening the speech (2/7)

- and he moves once more into three lines of non-embellishment as soon as the drums are heard (presumably, because of the dialogue, two lines earlier than as set in F)

The Life and Death of King John

French Herald

You men of Angiers open wide your gates,
2.1.300 - 311

English Herald

Rejoyce you men of Angiers, ring your bels,
2.1.312 - 324

Background: despite the blandishments and warnings in earlier speeches, the Citizens of Angiers still refuse to take sides, so both armies have left the stage to fight. After the first skirmish, Heralds from each side return to make remarkably similar claims of victory.

Style: both as large-scale public address

Where: outside Angiers

To Whom: to the Citizens above, standing on the walls

French Herald: # of Lines: 12

Probable Timing: 0.40 minutes

English Herald: # of Lines: 13

Probable Timing: 0.40 minutes

French Herald

1   You men of Angiers open wide your gates,
     And let young Arthur Duke of Britain in,
     Who by the hand of France this day hath made
     Much work for tears in many an English mother,
     Whose sons lie scattered on the bleeding ground .

2   Many a widows husband grovelling lies,
     Coldly embracing the discolored earth,
     And victory with little loss doth play
     Upon the dancing banners of the French,
     Who are at hand, triumphantly displayed,
     To enter conquerors, and to proclaim
     Arthur of [Britain] England's King and yours .

English Herald

1   Rejoice, you men of Angiers, ring your bells,
     King John, your King and England's, doth approach,
     Commander of this hot malicious day .

2   Their armors, that march'd hence so silver bright,
     Hither return all gilt with Frenchmen's blood .

3   There stuck no plume in any English crest
     That is removed by a staff of France ;
     Our colors do return in those same hands
     That did display them when we first march'd forth ;
     And like a jolly troop of huntsmen come
     Our lusty English, all with purpled hands,
     Dy'd in the dying slaughter of their foes .

5   Open your gates and give the victors way .

French Herald

1　You men of Angiers open wide your gates,
　And let yong Arthur Duke of Britaine in,
　Who by the hand of France, this day hath made
　Much worke for teares in many an English mother,
　Whose sonnes lye scattered on the bleeding ground :
　Many a widdowes husband groveling lies,
　Coldly embracing the discoloured earth,
　And victorie with little losse doth play
　Upon the dancing banners of the French,
　Who are at hand triumphantly displayed
　To enter Conquerors, and to proclaime
　Arthur of [Britaine], Englands King, xand yours .

English Herald

1　Rejoyce you men of Angiers, ring your bels,
　King John, your king and Englands, doth approach,
　Commander of this hot malicious day,
　Their Armours that march'd hence so silver bright,
　Hither returne all gilt with Frenchmens blood :
　There stucke no plume in any English Crest,
　That is removed by a staffe of France .

2　Our colours do returne in those same hands
　That did display them when we first marcht forth :
　And like a jolly troope of Huntsmen come
　Our lustie English, all with purpled hands,
　Dide in the dying slaughter of their foes,
　Open your gates, and give the Victors way .

As with the English counterpart below, F's orthography splits the speech neatly into three parts, and so there's a much better public address build set as just one sentence instead of most modern texts' two.

- the first two lines to associate themselves with Arthur are purely intellectual (4/0)

- the following six lines of boasting that England is defeated are highly emotional (2/7)

- while the final four line summation is once more splendidly mentally disciplined (6/2)

- two interesting sidebars in the summary : the third line from the end is spoken much faster without the added modern commas, while there is a much greater flourish of command in the last line if the extra breath-thought set only in F is utilized

As with his French counterpart above, F's orthography splits the speech neatly into three parts, and so there's a much better public address build as just two sentences instead of most modern texts' four.

- the first three lines to celebrate the English victory are highly intellectual (4/1)

- removing the two added modern text commas in the first sentence (lines 1 and 4) allows the herald more enthusiastic speed than is set for the modern counterpart

- the reporting of the gory glory of the supposed English victory becomes passionate, with slightly more emphasis on the emotional (5/6, the last four lines of F #1 and the opening two lines of F #2)

- and while the passion remains in the final four lines of F #2 it becomes slightly more intellectually controlled (3/2)

- and once more there is a final extra breath-thought in the last line, allowing once again a more heraldic flourish finish to the speech

The Life and Death of King John

Arthur

Must you with hot Irons, burne out both mine eyes?

between 4.1.39 - 56

Background: Hubert has a warrant from John to burn out Arthur's eyes. The following are Arthur's eventually successful attempts to dissuade Hubert from carrying out John's orders.

Style: both as part of a two-handed scene

Where: unspecified, most modern texts suggesting 'a room in a castle'

To Whom: Hubert

# of Lines: 17

Probable Timing: 0.55 minutes

Take Note: Not surprisingly, the speech is riddled with emotion (3/16 throughout), yet given the appalling circumstances, at times Arthur still manages to display an amazing mastery of rhetorical argument.

Arthur

1   Must you with hot irons burn out both mine eyes?

---

2   Have you the heart?

3   When your head did but
     ache,
     I knit my handkercher about your brows
     (The best I had, a princess wrought it me)
     And I did never ask it you again ;
     And with my hand at midnight held your head ;
     And like the watchful minutes to the hour,
     Still and anon cheer'd up the heavy time,
     Saying, "What lack you?" and "Where lies your grief ?"
     Or "What good love may I perform for you?"

4   Many a poor man's son would have lien still,
     And ne'er have spoke a loving word to you ;
     But you at your sick service had a prince .

5   Nay, you may think my love was crafty love,
     And call it cunning .

6   Do, and if you will ;
     If heaven be pleas'd that you must use me ill,
     Why then you must .

Arthur

1   Must you with hot Irons, burne out both mine eyes?

---

2   Have you the heart?

3   When your head did but
ake,
I knit my hand-kercher about your browes
(The best I had, a Princesse wrought it me)
And I did never aske it you againe :
And with my hand, at midnight held your head ;
And like the watchfull minutes, to the houre,
Still and anon cheer'd up the heavy time ;
Saying, what lacke you? and where lies your greefe?
Or what good love may I performe for you?

4   Many a poore mans sonne would have lyen still,
And nere have spoke a loving word to you :
But you, at your sicke service had a Prince :
Nay, you may thinke my love was craftie love,
And call it cunning .

5   Do, and if you will,
If heaven be pleas'd that you must use me ill,
Why then you must .

- the two short sentences opening the speech are absolutely to the point, and the F only extra breath-thought in F #1 (marked ,) makes even more poignant the questioning of the revolting action ending the line

- if 'Irons' is regarded as one syllable (which poets argue is metrically correct), then the two sentences are even more demanding in that they are monosyllabic too

- the one surround phrase ' : But you at your sicke service had a Prince : ' brilliantly reminds Hubert of the social gap between them, one that Hubert should not be betraying

- yet the strain keeps breaking through quite noticeably, as with the two (emotional) semicolons which remind both of them how close they were when Arthur 'at midnight held your head;' and 'cheer'd up the heavy time;' during Hubert's recent illness: and there is the one onrush of F #4 pushing together three strands as one (a 'poore mans sonne' wouldn't have done what I did; and but you 'had a Prince' but you may think 'my love was craftie love') the latter of which most modern texts regard should syntactically be set as a separate sentence (mt. #5), denying Arthur's slight urgency and/or loss of control at this point

- quite remarkably, the whole of F's last sentence is both non-embellished and monosyllabic ('heaven' again being treated as one syllable) – perhaps suggesting that the horror of the situation has struck home so much that Arthur has no more energy left or is simply too frightened to protest any more

The Life and Death of King John

Arthur

Will you put out mine eyes?
between 4.1.56 - 83

Background: Hubert has a warrant from John to burn out Arthur's eyes. The following are Arthur's eventually successful attempts to dissuade Hubert from carrying out John's orders.

Style: both as part of a two-handed scene

Where: unspecified, most modern texts suggesting 'a room in a castle'

To Whom: Hubert, with the last two sentences of the speech triggered by Hubert's calling in the executioners

# of Lines: 20

Probable Timing: 1.00 minutes

Take Note: F's orthography and sentence structure reveal that now Arthur's struggle between control and emotional breakdown is even more marked

Arthur

1   Will you put out mine eyes,
     These eyes that never did, nor never shall
     So much as frown on you ?

_____

2   Ah, none but in this iron age would do it !

3   The iron of itself, though heat red hot,
     Approaching near these eyes, would drink my tears,
     And quench [his] fiery indignation
     Even in the matter of mine innocence ;
     Nay, after that, consume away in rust,
     But for containing fire to harm mine eye .

4   Are you more stubborn-hard [than] hammer'd iron?

5   And if an angel should have come to me
     And told me Hubert should put out mine eyes,
     I would not have believ'd him - no tongue but Hubert's .

_____

6   Alas, what need you be so boist'rous-rough?

_____

7   I will not struggle, I will stand stone-still . {†}

8   And I will sit as quiet as a lamb;
     I will not stir, not [wince], nor speak a word,
     Nor look upon the iron angerly {:†} I'll forgive you,
     What ever torment you do put me to .

Arthur

1　Will you put out mine eyes?

2　These eyes, that never did, nor never shall
　　So much as frowne on you .

3　Ah, none but in this Iron Age, would do it :
　　The Iron of it selfe, though heate red hot,
　　Approaching neere these eyes, would drinke my teares,
　　And quench [this] fierie indignation,
　　Even in the matter of mine innocence :
　　Nay, after that, consume away in rust,
　　But for containing fire to harme mine eye :
　　Are you more stubborne hard, [then] hammer'd Iron?

4　And if an Angell should have come to me,
　　And told me Hubert should put out mine eyes,
　　I would not have beleev'd him : no tongue but Huberts .

5　Alas, what neede you be so boistrous rough?

6　I will not struggle, I will stand stone still : {†}
　　And I will sit as quiet as a Lambe .

7　I will not stirre, not [winch], nor speake a word,
　　Nor looke upon the Iron angerly { : †} Ile forgive you,
　　What ever torment you do put me too .

- whereas modern texts open with a one sentence, three line, single, seem-ingly emotional, question, F, by splitting mt. #1 in two, suggests Arthur is still in rhetorical control, asking a quicker question (F #1) and then defining what it would be that Hubert would be betraying/injuring

- in contrast, the onrush of F #3 suggests Arthur's control doesn't last, yet surprisingly here most modern texts create a far more rational character by hiving off the opening and closing lines as separate one line sentences

  a/ mt. #2 becomes more of a comment instead of F's statement as the first point of an extended debate

  b/ mt. #4 becomes a separate logical question, whereas F sets the same line as a built-to, inevitable question springing out of the previous seven lines without pause

- and though each text sets the last five lines as two sentences, their respective structures (and effect) are very different: modern texts offer a single line (mt. #7) of seeming dignity and then a four line elaboration (mt. #8) which seems somehow to undo the dignity: F, on the other hand, offers a much firmer two line statement of intent since both lines are surround phrases (F #6) and then, thanks to F's orthography, while the final three line elaboration (F #7) may start emotionally (1/3), the final line and a half is amazingly calm given the circumstances - not only is it non-embellished until the final word ('too') it is (almost) a surround phrase as well

- that emotions dominate this struggle is seen with capitals outbal-anced by long spellings (8/15 overall) - the capitals only dominating lines 1-2 of F #3 (the word play on 'Iron', 3/2) and the clever argu-ment that not even an angel could convince him of what Hubert is about to do (3/2, F #4)

- while six colons suggest a fiercely logical Arthur, the five extra breath-thoughts in F #2-4 suggest that he needs extra time to maintain self-control and to persuade Hubert not to blind him

The Life and Death of King Richard the Second

Captain/Captaine

My Lord of Salisbury, we have stayd ten dayes,
between 2.4.1 - 17

Background: the only scene for the Welsh Captaine, a pragmatic supporter of Richard; as such the speech, given to one of Richard's leading supporters, is self-explanatory.

Style: as part of a two-handed scene

Where: unspecified, but presumably a camp somewhere in or near Wales

To Whom: Salisbury, one of Richard's generals

# of Lines: 15

Probable Timing: 0.50 minutes

Take Note: Though the Captaine's only speech in the play, F's orthography, with no fewer than four (emotional) semicolons, and two onrushed sentences, suggests that the parting is quite an emotional event for him.

Captain

1   My Lord of Salisbury, we have stay'd ten days,
    And hardly kept our countrymen together,
    And yet we hear no tidings from the King,
    Therefore we will disperse our selves {†} .

---

2   'Tis thought the King is dead ; we will not stay .

3   The bay-trees in our country [are all] wither'd,
    And meteors fright the fixed stars of heaven,
    The pale-fac'd moon looks bloody on the earth,
    And lean-look'd prophets whisper fearful change,
    Rich men look sad, and ruffians dance and leap,
    The one in fear to lose what they enjoy,
    The other to enjoy by rage, and war .

4   These signs forerun the death [or fall] of kings .

5   Farewell !

6   Our countrymen are gone and fled,
    As well assur'd Richard their king is dead .

Captaine

1   My Lord of Salisbury, we have stayd ten dayes,
    And hardly kept our Countreymen together,
    And yet we heare no tidings from the King ;
    Therefore we will disperse our selves {†} .

---

2   'Tis thought the King is dead, we will not stay ;
    The Bay-trees in our Countrey [all are] wither'd,
    And Meteors fright the fixed Starres of Heaven ;
    The pale-fac'd Moone lookes bloody on the Earth,
    And leane-look'd Prophets whisper fearefull change ;
    Rich men looke sad, and Ruffians dance and leape,
    The one in feare, to loose what they enjoy,
    The other to enjoy by Rage, and Warre :
    These signes fore-run the death [ ] of Kings .

3   Farewell, our Countreymen are gone and fled,
    As well assur'd Richard their King is dead .

- the nub of the speech is very clear from the first surround phrase, doubly heightened by the fact that it is non-embellished and set up by an (emotional) semicolon

     " ; Therefore we will disperse our selves . "

- and the other semicoloned and essentially non-embellished phrase (save for the capitalized 'King') explains why

     " . tis thought the King is dead, we will not stay ; "

  the final surround phrase explaining the reason for the belief

     " : These signs fore-run the death of Kings . "

- the speech opens passionately (F #1, 4/3), with the announcement of departure being, as noted, unembellished as if it were a decision that will not be changed by any contrary argument

- the first three lines of onrushed F #2 explaining why are firmly intellectual (6/1), while passion colours his explanation of the bulk of the 'Portents' (7/9 for the rest of the sentence) – the passion and the onrush all pointing to less rhetorical control than modern texts would like, most of which split the sentence in three

- but mental discipline is regained for the final farewell couplet (F #3, 3/1)

The Life and Death of
King Richard the Second

Gardener/Gardiner

Hold thy peace ./{The King} that hath suffer'd this disorder'd Spring,

between 3.4.48 - 71

Background: one of the 'Gardiner's' servants, expanding on a metaphor that compares the Duke of Yorke's garden that they are working on to all of England, has voiced the worrying question as to why should they try to keep the real garden in order when the country at large 'is full of weedes' and 'her wholesome Hearbes/Swarming with Caterpillars' - an obvious reference to the wasteful behaviour of Richard and his coterie. This triggers the speech.

Style: as part of a three handed scene, in front of a small unobserved group of listeners

Where: in the garden of the Duke of Yorke's home at Langley

To Whom: the two servants, with the unobserved Queene and her two Ladies also listening

# of Lines: 23 Probable Timing: 1.10 minutes

Take Note: Both F and the quarto set an irregular passage (shown shaded here) for the news of Richard's capture (10/12/13 syllables), the emphasis on the final two lines suggesting that the gardening analogy is what is most important for the Gardiner and his colleagues, i.e. bringing the incident down into a world where they can understand it. Some modern texts remove the emphasis by the rather inelegant restructuring of a short line, usually four syllables (here expanded to six for the logical flow of the speech), followed by one irregular line (12 syllables) and two normal ones (10/10), which removes the emphasis on the gardening image and places it simply on the news of the capture. (The importance of the capture is still marked in F by the five extra breath-thoughts in this section alone .)

Background

Gardener

1   Hold thy peace .

2   {The King} that hath suffered this disordered spring,
     Hath now himself met with the fall of leaf .

3   The weeds that his broad-spreading leaves did shelter,
     That seem'd in eating him to hold him up,
     Are [pluck'd] up root and all by Bullingbrook,
     I mean the Earl of Wiltshire, Bushy, Green { }
     {Are dead}, and Bullingbrook
     Hath seiz'd the wasteful King .

4   O, what pity is it
     That he had not so trimm'd and dress'd his land
     As we this garden !

5   {We}at time of year,
     [Do] wound the bark, the skin of our fruit-trees,
     [Lest] being over-proud [in] sap and blood,
     With too much riches it confound itself ;
     Had he done so to great and growing men,
     They might have liv'd to bear and he to taste
     Their fruits of duty .

6   Superfluous branches
     We lop away, that bearing boughs may live ;
     Had he done so, himself had born the crown,
     Which waste [of] idle hours hath quite thrown down .

7   Depress'd he is already, and depos'd
     'Tis [doubt] he will be .

8   Letters came last night
     To a dear friend of the [good] Duke of York's
     That tell black tidings .

Gardiner

1 Hold thy peace .

2 {The King} that hath suffer'd this disorder'd Spring,
Hath now himselfe met with the Fall of Leafe .

3 The Weeds that his broad-spreading Leaves did shelter,
That seem'd, in eating him, to hold him up,
Are [pull'd up], Root and all, by Bullingbrooke :
I meane, the Earle of Wiltshire, Bushie, Greene {are dead},
And Bullingbrooke hath seiz'd the wastefull King .

4 Oh, what pitty is it, that he had not so trim'd
And drest his Land, as we this Garden, { } at time of yeare,
[And] wound the Barke, the skin of our Fruit-trees,
[Least] being over-proud [with] Sap and Blood,
With too much riches it confound it selfe ?

5 Had he done so, to great and growing men,
They might have liv'd to beare, and he to taste
Their fruites of dutie .

6   Superfluous branches
We lop away, that bearing boughes may live :
Had he done so, himselfe had borne the Crowne,
Which waste [and] idle houres, hath quite thrown downe .

Deprest he is already, and depos'd
'Tis [doubted] he will be .

8   Letters came last night
To a deere Friend of the [ ] Duke of Yorkes,
That tell blacke tydings .

- following the terse command to one of his underlings not to speak out of turn (triply unusual in being short, unembellished, and monosyllabic, perhaps suggesting that he regards what has been said or how it has been said as offensive), the Gardiner informs his colleagues quite factually as to the King's capture and his cronies being, using gardening images, 'pull'd up' (8/2 in F #2 and the first three lines of F #3)

- then passion breaks through as he wishes Richard had employed as good a husbandry for the country as they do for their garden (12/10 in the two lines ending F #3 and five lines of F #4)

- though emotional, the regret of F #5 seems much quieter (and genuine?) (0/2), though describing how Richard might have taken care of England (his 'garden') releases great emotion in him (1/6, F #6)

- the quietness returns once more as he realises Richard's bleak future, for F #7 is the only non-embellished sentence in the speech

- for some reason his passions come to the fore (a supporter of Richard perhaps, since he describes the news as 'black tydings') as he explains how he comes to know all this (3/4, in the two lines of F #8) F's onrushed single sentence and orthography suggest that the Gardiner maintains a passionate sustained release (8/11, heightened by the three rhyming couplets) as he makes plans to redesign part of the garden to commemorate the Queene's visit (sympathy for her driving him on perhaps). By dividing it into three sentences most modern texts make the small speech reflective rather than active.

The Life and Death of
King Richard the Second

Richard

Musicke do I heare ?
5.5.41 - 66

Background: instead of the Tower, Richard has been incarcerated well away from London in the northern Castle of Pomfret (more usually known as Pontefrect) in West Yorkshire, thus separating him even further from any London support and his wife, now exiled in France. This speech continues directly from his speech which deals with the way Richard is trying to cope with his imprisonment, while in this speech he comes to an unenviable understanding of what his past life has led to.

Style: so Where: a dungeon in Pomfret Castle

To Whom: direct audience address and self

# of Lines: 26

Probable Timing: 1.20

Take Note: As the music starts, Richard finally has a single topic around which his hitherto whirling thoughts can centre, as the opening short sentence 'Musicke do I heare?' and the surround phrases show.

Richard

1   Music do I hear ?

2   Ha, ha ?keep time !

3   How sour sweet music is
     When time is broke, and no proportion kept !

4   So is it in the music of men's lives .

5   And here have I the daintiness of ear
     To [check] time broke in a disorder'd string ;
     But for the concord of my state and time
     Had not an ear to hear my true time broke .

6   I wasted time, and now doth time waste me ;
     For now hath time made me his numb'ring clock:
     My thoughts are minutes, and with sighs they jar
     Their watches on unto mine eyes, the outward watch,
     Whereto my finger, like a dial's point,
     Is pointing still, in cleansing them from tears.

7   Now, sir, the sound that tells what hour it is,
     Are clamorous groans, [which] strike upon my heart,
     Which is the bell .

8   So sighs, and tears, and groans,
     Show minutes, [times, and hours] : but my time
     Runs posting on in Bullingbrook's proud joy,
     While I stand fooling here, his Jack [of the] clock.

9   This music mads me, let it sound no more,
     For though it have holp madmen to their wits,
     In me it seems it will make wise men mad .

10   Yet blessing on his heart that gives it me !
     For 'tis a sign of love ; and love to Richard
     Is a strange brooch in this all-hating world .

Richard

1 Musicke do I heare ?

2 Ha, ha ? keepe time : How sowre sweet Musicke is,
   When Time is broke, and no Proportion kept ?

3 So is it in the Musicke of mens lives :
   And heere have I the daintinesse of eare,
   To [heare] time broke in a disorder'd string :
   But for the Concord of my State and Time,
   Had not an eare to heare my true Time broke .

4 I wasted Time, and now doth Time waste me :
   For now hath Time made me his numbring clocke ;
   My Thoughts, are minutes ; and with Sighes they jarre,
   Their watches on unto mine eyes, the outward Watch,
   Whereto my finger, like a Dialls point,
   Is pointing still, in cleansing them from teares .

5 Now sir, the sound that tels what houre it is,
   Are clamorous groanes, [that] strike upon my heart,
   Which is the bell :so Sighes, and Teares, and Grones,
   Shew Minutes, [Houres, and Times] : but my Time
   Runs poasting on, in Bullingbrookes proud joy,
   While I stand fooling heere, his jacke [o'th]'Clocke .

6 This Musicke mads me, let it sound no more,
   For though it have holpe madmen to their wits,
   In me it seemes, it will make wise-men mad :
   Yet blessing on his heart that gives it me ;
   For 'tis a signe of love, and love to Richard,
   Is a strange Brooch, in this all-hating world .

- the first surround phrases show the progression of Richard's thinking
  " . Ha, ha ? keepe time : How sowre sweet Musicke is,/When Time is broke, and no Proportion kept ? /So is it in the Musicke of mens lives : "
  " . I wasted Time, and now doth Time waste me : /For now hath Time made me his numbring clocke ; /My Thoughts, are minutes ; "
  " : so Sighes, and Teares, and Grones,/Shew Minutes, Houres, and Times : " while the last ' : Yet blessing on his heart that gives it me ;' suggests that thinking of someone other than himself for the first time in sixty lines Richard may have reached some form of equilibrium, especially since the line is also non-embellished and in part formed by an (emotional) semicolon

- even so, there is still much quick shifting in styles in a series of onrushed sentences (F #2, #3, #5, and #6) which, as set in F, add to Richard's still whirling confusion: most modern texts reduce this by splitting each sentence into a more grammatical series of two sentences each

- as the music is first heard Richard responds emotionally (0/3, F #1 and the first phrase of F #2)

- then, realising the connection between 'Musicke' and 'mens lives', so his passion comes to the fore (5/4 the remainder of F #2, and the first line of #3)

- F #3's next two lines cursing himself for being able to hear discords is emotional (0/4), but then applying the discord to his own life and realising how he wasted time returns to intellect (7/3, in the finish to F #3 and the first two lines of F #4), and the expansion of his wasting 'Time' becomes passionate (4/4 to the end of F #4)

- and still the shifting styles continue, with his groans counting time being emotionally expressed (0/2 in the first two and a half lines of F #5), followed by an immensely passionate release as all his grieving is equated with his accounting for things gone by (6/5 in just the single surround phrase)

- and as this brings him back to realizing how he allowed himself to be Bullingbrooke's 'jacke o'th'Clocke' (the last two and a half lines of F #5) and momentarily begs the music to stop (the first three lines of F #6) so emotion breaks through (3/8), which he seems able to hold in check, first by leading to the non-embellished blessing, as discussed above, and then, finally, intellect alone in the last line and a half of the speech

The First Part of
Henry the Fourth

Sir Richard Vernon

The Earle of Westmerland, seven thousand strong,
between 4.1.88 - 110

Background: this is the first speech in the play for one of the chief rebels, Sir Richard Vernon. As both a report of the King's forces facing them and an assessment of the new self-presentation of the former 'Mad-Cap Prince of Wales', i.e. Hal, the speech is self-explanatory.

Style: general report to a small group

Where: the rebels camp near Shrewsbury

To Whom: Hotspurre, Worcester, Dowglas (leader of the Scots), and perhaps a Messenger

# of Lines: 19

Probable Timing: 1.00 minutes

Take Note: Once Vernon's excessive passion starts to flow (from the fourth line on in F #2), it's fascinating to realise that, except for one line, the bulk of his release comes at the end of the line or phrase, as if his speaking style and the reporting are inextricably intertwined.

Vernon

1　The Earl of Westmerland, seven thousand strong,
　　Is marching hitherwards, with [him] Prince John .

2　The King himself in person [is] set forth,
　　Or hitherwards intended speedily,
　　With strong and mighty preparation{Y}

　　All furnish'd, all in arms;
　　All plum'd like estridges, that with the wind
　　Baited like eagles having lately bath'd,
　　Glittering in golden coats like images,
　　As full of spirit as the month of May,
　　And gorgeous as the sun at midsummer ;
　　Wanton as youthful goats, wild as young bulls .

3　I saw young Harry with his beaver on,
　　His cushes on his thighs, gallantly arm'd,
　　Rise from the ground like feathered Mercury,
　　And vaulted with such ease into his seat
　　As if an angel dropp'd down from the clouds
　　To turn and wind a fiery Pegasus,
　　And witch the world with noble horsemanship .

Vernon

1 The Earle of Westmerland, seven thousand strong,
   Is marching hither-wards, with [ ] Prince John .

---

2 The King himselfe in person [hath] set forth,
   Or hither-wards intended speedily,
   With strong and mightie preparation{Y}

   All furnisht, all in Armes,
   All plum'd like Estridges, that with the Winde
   Bayted like Eagles, having lately bath'd,
   Glittering in Golden Coates, like Images,
   As full of spirit as the Moneth of May,
   And gorgeous as the Sunne at Mid-summer,
   Wanton as youthfull Goates, wilde as young Bulls .

3 I saw young Harry with his Bever on,
   His Cushes on his thighes, gallantly arm'd,
   Rise from the ground like feathered Mercury,
   And vaulted with such ease into his Seat,
   As if an Angell dropt downe from the Clouds,
   To turne and winde a fierie Pegasus,
   And witch the World with Noble Horsemanship .

- the two themes of the speech are clearly outlined in the non-embellished phrases as both being of key concern

  a/ the quick advance of the Royalist forces
     " . . . hither-wards intended speedily,/With strong and mightie preparation, All furnisht . . . "

  b/ the presence of Hal, 'gallantly arm'd,'

- that Vernon is impressed (whether in admiration or fear) by the opposition forces can be seen in the four extra breath-thoughts the 'Eagle' imagery of the royalist forces in F #2, and the 'Angell/Pegasus' of Hal (F #3)

- the bare facts of the smaller units of the Royalist army (Westmerland and John) are reported strongly intellectually (4/1, F #1)

- however, the King's approach is reported much more carefully (1/1, F #2)

- but once F #2's detailed description of the royalists 'all in Armes' starts, there is a multitude of excess (13/9 in just the seven remaining lines)

- Vernon seems very struck by (the change in?) Hal, for F #3 initially starts out highly factual (5/1 in the first four lines), but emotion starts creeping back in with the extension of the description into Hal as an 'Angell' and his horse as 'Pegasus' (6/3 in the last three lines of the speech)

Chiefe Justice

I then did use the person of your Father :
5.2.73 - 101

Background: the Lord Chiefe Justice once had occasion to impris-on the new King when he was Prince of Wales. Challenged im-mediately by Hal, 'How might a Prince of my great hopes forget/ So great Indignities you laid upon me?', the following is the Lord Chiefe Justice's well reasoned reply.

Style: one on one for the benefit of the whole group

Where: the palace at Westminster

To Whom: Hal as the new King Henry V, as well as Hal's brothers John (Lancaster), Thomas (Clarence), and Humphrey (Gloucester); and Warwicke

# of Lines: 29

Probable Timing: 1.25 minutes

Take Note: Though sentences match, F's orthography outlines the awkward stages of the the Chiefe Justice's struggle as he attempts to justify himself with dignity to a new king he firmly believes an avowed enemy to him for actions the Justice had initiated against him in his wilder, younger days. The large number of extra breath-thoughts (sixteen, marked ,) and the sudden cluster of heavy punc-tuation in the last sentence point to a task far more difficult than most modern texts present.

Background

Chief Justice

1   I then did use the person of your father,
     The image of his power lay then in me,
     And in th'administration of his law,
     Whiles I was busy for the commonwealth,
     Your Highness pleased to forget my place,
     The majesty and power of law and justice,
     The image of the King whom I presented,
     And strook me in my very seat of judgment;
     Whereon (as an offender to your father)
     I gave bold way to my authority,
     And did commit you .

2   If the deed were ill,
     Be you contented, wearing now the garland,
     To have a son set your decrees at nought ?

3   To pluck down justice from your [aweful] bench ?

4   To trip the course of law and blunt the sword
     That guards the peace and safety of your person ?

5   Nay more, to spurn at your most royal image,
     And mock your workings in a second body ?

6   Question your royal thoughts, make the case yours ;
     Be now the father and propose a son,
     Hear your own dignity so much profan'd,
     See your most dreadful laws so loosely slighted,
     Behold your self so by a son disadained ;
     And then imagine me taking [your] part,
     And in your power soft silencing your son,
     After this cold considerance, sentence me,
     And, as you are a king, speak in your state
     What I have done that misbecame my place,
     My person, or my liege's sovereignty.

Chiefe Justice

1 I then did use the person of your Father :
The Image of his power, lay then in me,
And in th'administration of his Law,
Whiles I was busie for the Commonwealth,
Your Highnesse pleased to forget my place,
The Majesty, and power of Law, and Justice,
The Image of the King, whom I presented,
And strooke me in my very Seate of Judgement :
Whereon (as an Offender to your Father)
I gave bold way to my Authority,
And did commit you .

2   If the deed were ill,
Be you contented, wearing now the Garland,
To have a Sonne, set your Decrees at naught ?

3 To plucke downe justice from your[awfull] Bench ?

4 To trip the course of Law, and blunt the Sword,
That guards the peace, and safety of your Person ?

5 Nay more, to spurne at your most Royall Image,
And mocke your workings, in a Second body ?

6 Question your Royall Thoughts, make the case yours :
Be now the Father, and propose a Sonne :
Heare your owne dignity so much prophan'd,
See your most dreadfull Lawes, so loosely slighted ;
Behold your selfe, so by a Sonne disadained :
And then imagine me, taking [you] part,
And in your power, soft silencing your Sonne :
After this cold considerance, sentence me ;
And, as you are a King, speake in your State,
What I have done, that misbecame my place,
My person, or my Lieges Soveraigntie .

- since emotion very rarely outweighs his intellect, sentence F #3, dealing with the legal affronts Hal was then guilty of, should be seen as fundamental to the Chiefe Justice's passionate beliefs, doubly weighted by being the only short sentence in the speech: this can be coupled with the only other emotional passage in the speech, the two lines from the middle of F #6, the second line of which is a surround phrase, "See your most dreadfull Lawes, so loosely slighted ; /Behold your selfe, so by a Sonne disadained : "

- the surround phrases underscore the Justice's well-reasoned reply
  " . I then did use the person of your Father . "
  " . Question your Royall Thoughts, make the case yours : /Be now the Father, and propose a Sonne : "
  " : Behold your selfe, so by a Sonne disadained : "
  " : After this cold considerance, sentence me ; "

- not surprisingly, the speech starts out strongly intellectual, (18/5, F #1-2), though interestingly there are more extra breath-thoughts (five, all touching on the power that then lay in the Justice, and Hal's flouting of it) than major punctuation (two colons), suggesting that logic may not be the strong suite just yet

- following the already discussed short F #3, the Justice quickly regains enough composure to intellectually elaborate on Hal's further transgressions (F #4 3/0), yet now the extra breath-thoughts start to make themselves felt; as the descriptions turn to Hal's seemingly spurning his father, not only do these continue but the speech turns to passion (10/8, F #5 and the first seven lines of F #6, save the already mentioned second emotional break - 1/4 - in lines 3 and 4)

- and as this passion starts so does the clustering of major punctuation and extra breath thoughts throughout the final sentence, as if the passionate ending summarizing Hal's actions bursts forth from him, despite his attempts to rein himself in

- that the Justice eventually does establish self control (via a wonderful non-embellished surround phrase formed in part by an emotional semicolon), the final challenge of 'would you have done differently (4/1) in the last three lines, is an amazing testimony to his dignity and resilience

The Life of Henry the Fift

Boy

As young as I am, I have observ'd these three
3.2.28 - 53

Background: though Bardolph is eager to join in the battle at Harfleur, Nym and Pistoll insist on taking a 'safety' breather. The Welsh captain Fluellen has come across them, and with no sympathy whatsoever, has driven them into battle with 'Up to the breach, you Dogges; avaunt you Cullions', leaving Falstaffe's Boy with the following comments.

Style: solo

Where: close to the town of Harfleur

To Whom: direct audience address

# of Lines: 26

Probable Timing: 1.20 minutes

Take Note: While most modern texts set five rational sentences to open the speech, F sets the information as one long onrushed release, and it's only after this that the sentence structures begin to match – suggesting that as set in F the Boy cannot establish self-control straightaway.

Boy

1 As young as I am, I have observ'd these three
   swashers .

2   I am boy to them all three, but all they three,
   though they would serve me, could not be man to me ;
   for indeed three such [antics] do not amount to a man .

3 For Bardolph, he is white-liver'd, and red-fac'd ; by the
   means whereof a faces it out, but fights not .

4   For Pistol,
   he hath a killing tongue and a quiet sword ; by the
   means whereof a breaks words, and keeps whole
   weapons .

5   For [Nym], he hath heard, that men of few
   words are the best men, and therefore he scorns to say
   his prayers, lest a should be thought a coward ; but his
   few bad words are match'd with as few good deeds ; for
   a never broke any man's head but his own, and that was
   against a post when he was drunk .

6   They will steal any
   thing, and call it purchase .

7   Bardolph stole a lute-case,
   bore it twelve leagues, and sold it for three half -pence .

8 [Nym] and Bardolph are sworn brothers in filching, and
   in [Calais] they stole a fire-shovel .

9   I knew by that piece
   of service the men would carry coals .

10   They would
   have me as familiar with men's pockets as their gloves
   or their handkerchers ; which makes much against my
   manhood, if I should take from another's pocket to put
   into mine ; for it is plain pocketing up of wrongs .

11 I must leave them, and seek some better service .

12   Their
   villainy goes against my weak stomach, and therefore
   I must cast it up .

Boy

1 As young as I am, I have observ'd these three
Swashers : I am Boy to them all three, but all they three,
though they would serve me, could not be Man to me ;
for indeed three such [Antiques] doe not amount to a man :
for Bardolph, hee is white-liver'd, and red-fac'd ; by the
meanes whereof, a faces it out, but fights not : for Pistoll,
hee hath a killing Tongue, and a quiet Sword ; by the
meanes whereof, a breakes Words, and keepes whole
Weapons : for [Nim], hee hath heard, that men of few
Words are the best men, and therefore hee scornes to say
his Prayers, lest a should be thought a Coward : but his
few bad Words are matcht with as few good Deeds ; for
a never broke any mans Head but his owne, and that was
against a Post, when he was drunke .

2   They will steale any
thing, and call it Purchase .

3   Bardolph stole a Lute-case,
bore it twelve Leagues, and sold it for three halfepence .

4 [Nim] and Bardolph are sworne Brothers in filching : and
in [Callice] they stole a fire-shovell .

5   I knew by that peece
of Service, the men would carry Coales .

6   They would
have me as familiar with mens Pockets, as their Gloves
or their Hand-kerchers : which makes much against my
Manhood, if I should take from anothers Pocket, to put
into mine ; for it is plaine pocketting up of Wrongs .

7 I must leave them, and seeke some better Service : their
Villany goes against my weake stomacke, and therefore
I must cast it up .

- this coupled with nine major pieces of punctuation (including four emotional semicolons), in this the opening sentence indicates that the Boy is undergoing some sort of profound self-exploration

- all of the surround phrases, save for the first that opens the speech, deal with the less than admirable qualities of Bardolph, Pistoll, and Nym

- the other surround phrases point to where the Boy is heading, viz. '. As young as I am, I have observ'd these three Swashers : ' followed by his description of their actions as ' ; for it is plaine pocketting up of Wrongs . ' leading to the inevitable conclusion ' . I must leave them, and seeke some better Service : '

- the Boy starts out intellectually (4/0 in the first four lines of F #1), and then while his intellect still functions during his assessment of each character, emotions come to the surface too (Bardolph 1/2; Pistoll, 5/5; Nym, 8/5)

- while the acknowledgement of their thievery in general is passionate (F #2, 1/1, F #5 2/2), the listing of their particular filching - F #3-4 - becomes intellectual once more (7/3), as is his concern that they want him to become a thief too (6/2, F #6)

- however, his recognition that he must 'seeke some better Service' becomes a passionate decision (2/3, F #7)

The Life of Henry the Fift

Mountjoy

Thus sayes my King : Say thou to Harry
3.6.118 - 136

Background: at first the French seem to have underestimated the English, but no longer; in an earlier scene the French King has called for all forces to assemble, and has sent the herald Mountjoy to warn Henry to pull back or be annihilated. The following is the first of several such visits by Mountjoy.

Style: one on one address for the benefit of all who are listening

Where: the English encampment

To Whom: King Henry, in front of his brother Humfrey (Gloucester), the captains Gower and Fluellen, and 'his poore souldiers'

# of Lines: 19

Probable Timing: 1.00 minutes

Take Note: F's orthography suggests that Mountjoy (the herald) is far more personally involved in the message he is delivering than might normally be expected. The combination of prose, giving the appearance of everyday behaviour, with such a careful build up via skilful use of the surround phrases presents the intriguing possibility that Mountjoy is taking things quite calmly, convinced that, whatever the reaction, he knows he will have performed his task well.

Mountjoy

1   Thus says my King : Say thou to Harry
    of England, Though we seem'd dead, we did but sleep;
    advantage is a better soldier [than] rashness.

2   Tell him
    we could have rebuk'd him at [Harfleur], but that we
    thought not good to bruise an injury till it were full
    ripe .

3   Now we speak upon our [cue], and our voice is im-
    perial : England shall repent his folly, see his weak-
    ness, and admire our sufferance .

4   Bid him therefore con-
    sider of his ransom, which must proportion the losses we
    have borne, the subjects we have lost, the disgrace we
    have digested ; which in weight to re-answer, his petti-
    ness would bow under .

5   For our losses, his exchequer is
    too poor ; for th'effusion of our blood, the muster of his
    kingdom too faint a number ; and for our disgrace, his
    own person kneeling at our feet but a weak and worth-
    less satisfaction .

6   To this add defiance ; and tell him, for
    conclusion, he hath betray'd his followers, whose con-
    demnation is pronounc'd .

7   So far my King and master ;
    so much my office .

Mountjoy

1   Thus sayes my King : Say thou to Harry
of England, Though we seem'd dead, we did but sleepe :
Advantage is a better Souldier [then] rashnesse .

2   Tell him,
wee could have rebuk'd him at [Harflewe], but that wee
thought not good to bruise an injurie, till it were full
ripe .

3   Now wee speake upon our [Q .] and our voyce is imperiall : England shall repent his folly, see his weake-
nesse, and admire our sufferance .

4   Bid him therefore con-
sider of his ransome, which must proportion the losses we
have borne, the subjects we have lost, the disgrace we
have digested ; which in weight to re-answer, his petti-
nesse would bow under .

5   For our losses, his Exchequer is
too poore ; for th'effusion of our bloud, the Muster of his
Kingdome too faint a number ; and for our disgrace, his
owne person kneeling at our feet, but a weake and worth-
lesse satisfaction .

6   To this adde defiance : and tell him for
conclusion, he hath betrayed his followers, whose condemnation is pronounc't : So farre my King and Master ;
so much my Office .

- however, to offset the apparent confidence, while the start and finish is handled with fine mental self-control (11/5, F #1 and the last two phrases ending the speech), the intervening handling of the message is surprisingly emotional (6/17)

- in addition, while the speech opens with three logical colons, for some reason it finishes with four emotional semicolons out of the last six pieces of major punctuation: they come at the end of an idea, suggesting that each point being made - Henry's Exchequer could not pay for the damage he has caused to France; nor the destroying of his men (the 'Muster') for the blood he has spilled; nor even Henry kneeling at the foot of the French King for the disgrace he has inflicted upon France; and the final defiance, cause Mountjoy distress, either as a Frenchman, or, and probably less likely, out of concern that, once delivered, his message may cause a dangerously adverse reaction towards him from Henry

- the final non-embellished lines suggest a very somber message beneath the fine rhetorical bluster, viz. "and tell him for conclusion, he hath betrayed his followers, whose condemnation is pronounc't:"

Boy

I did never know so full a voyce issue from so emptie
4.5.67 - 77

Background: another less than flattering assessment of Pistoll, made this time after Pistoll has brow-beaten a French prisoner into paying him a large sum of money for sparing his life. One note; sadly, the last sentence proves prophetic, for the boy is killed with all the others (directly against the rules of warfare) when the French invade the unprotected English camp while all the English soldiers are engaged elsewhere in battle.

Style: solo

Where: part of the battlefield at Agincourt

To Whom: direct audience address

# of Lines: 10

Probable Timing: 0.35 minutes

Take Note: As with the Boy's prior speech, by splitting each of F's onrushed sentences in two, most modern texts create a character much more rational and more capable of handling himself than F would suggest.

Boy

1   I did never know so full a voice issue from so empty a
    heart ; but the saying is true, "The empty vessel makes the
    greatest sound ."

2   [Bardolph] and Nym had ten times more
    valor [than] this roaring devil i'th old play, that every
    one may pare his nails with a wooden dagger, and
    they are both hang'd, and so would this be, if he durst
    steal any thing adventurously .

3   I must stay with the
    lackeys with the luggage of our camp .

4   The French might
    have a good [prey] of us, if he knew of it, for there is none
    to guard it but boys .

Boy

1   I did never know so full a voyce issue from so emptie a
heart : but the saying is true, The empty vessel makes the
greatest sound, [Bardolfe] and Nym had tenne times more
valour, [then] this roaring divell i'th olde play, that everie
one may payre his nayles with a woodden dagger, and
they are both hang'd, and so would this be, if hee durst
steale any thing adventurously .

2   I must stay with the
Lackies with the luggage of our camp, the French might
have a good [pray] of us, if he knew of it, for there is none
to guard it but boyes .

- his complete realisation of Pistoll's nature is underscored by the sentence opening with the surround phrase ' . I did never know so full a voyce issue from so emptie a heart : '

- the onrushed, fulsome, non-flattering description of Pistoll is highly emotional (3/10, F #1)

- however, by the time of telling the audience that he 'must stay with the Lackies' his emotions are well under control (2/1, F #2)

Herald {Mountjoy}

No great King :/I come to thee for charitable License,
between 4.7.70 - 85

Background: Mountjoy, the French Herald, has appeared for the third time. Not knowing the result of the current battle, Henry demands 'what meanes this Herald? knowst thou not/That I have fin'd these bones for ransome?/Com'st thou againe for ransome?'. The following is Mountjoy's surprising reply.

Style: one on one address, for the information of all who are listening

Where: the English encampment near Agincourt

To Whom: King Henry, with Prisoners, Exeter, brother Humfrey (Gloucester), and the Captains Fluellen and Gower

# of Lines: 14

Probable Timing: 0.50 minutes

Take Note: The small cracks in F's rhetorical setting reveal where the Herald has difficulty in controlling himself.

Herald

1 No, great King ;
I come to thee for charitable license,
That we may wander o'er this bloody field
To book our dead, and then to bury them ;
To sort our nobles from our common men .

2 For many of our princes (woe the while !)
Lie drown'd and soak'd in mercenary blood ;
So do our vulgar drench their peasant limbs
In blood of princes, and [their] wounded steeds
Fret fetlock deep in gore, and with wild rage
Yerk out their armed heels at their dead masters,
Killing them twice .

3   O, give us leave, great King,
To view the field in safety, and dispose
Of their dead bodies!

---

4   The day is yours .

Herald

1   No great King :
    I come to thee for charitable License,
    That we may wander ore this bloody field,
    To booke our dead, and then to bury them,
    To sort our Nobles from our common men .

2   For many of our Princes (woe the while)
    Lye drown'd and soak'd in mercenary blood :
    So do our vulgar drench their peasant limbes
    In blood of Princes, and [with] wounded steeds
    Fret fet-locke deepe in gore, and with wilde rage
    Yerke out their armed heeles at their dead masters,
    Killing them twice .

3   O give us leave great King,
    To view the field in safety, and dispose
    Of their dead bodies .

_____

4   The day is yours .

- at times the Herald speaks faster than most modern texts allow with their extra punctuation (shown in F as), thus the appeal of the first line of the last sentence has far more emotional weight to it as set in F

- the extra breath at the end of line three of F #1, and the setting of a comma instead of the modern text's semicolon again suggests a man who needs breath for self-control rather than one who can handle himself with the rhetorical ease he displayed earlier

- given that the character is attuned to self-control in public, the fact that he starts and finishes with mental self-control (3/1, F #1 and a very subdued 1/0, F #3) is not surprising

- thus the sudden emotional rush as he describes the mixture of bodies, some twice-killed by their horses, is worthy of note (2/7, F #2)

Chorus

Thus farre with rough, and all-unable Pen,
Epilogue 1 - 14

Background: the last speech of the play, as such it is self-explanatory.

Style: solo

Where: the theatre

To Whom: direct address

# of Lines: 14

Probable Timing: 0.50 minutes

As with the opening speech, this finale to the play is also highly intellectual (22/8)

Chorus

1   Thus far, with rough and all-unable pen,
     Our bending author hath pursu'd the story,
     In little room confining mighty men,
     Mangling by starts the full course of their glory .

2   Small time ; but in that small most greatly lived
     This star of England .

3   Fortune made his sword ;
     By which the world's best garden he achieved,
     And of it left his son imperial lord .

4   Henry the Sixt, in infant bands crown'd King
     Of France and England, did this king succeed ;
     Whose state so many had the managing,
     That they lost France, and made his England bleed ;
     Which oft our stage hath shown; and for their sake,
     In your fair minds let this acceptance take .

Chorus

1　　Thus farre with rough, and all-unable Pen,
　　　Our bending Author hath pursu'd the Story,
　　　In little roome confining mightie men,
　　　Mangling by starts the full course of their glory .

2　　Small time : but in that small, most greatly lived
　　　This Starre of England .

3　　　　　　　　　　　　　　　Fortune made his Sword ;
　　　By which, the Worlds best Garden he atchieved :
　　　And of it left his Sonne Imperiall Lord .

4　　Henry the Sixt, in Infant Bands crown'd King
　　　Of France and England, did this King succeed :
　　　Whose State so many had the managing,
　　　That they lost France, and made his England bleed :
　　　Which oft our Stage hath showne ; and for their sake,
　　　In your faire minds let this acceptance take .

- in view of how much territory, political alliance, and hope won in this play were wasted under Henry's infant son (Henry VI), the fact that all of sentences F #2-3, referring to the greatness of Henry the Fifth's reign, are composed of nothing but surround phrases, might suggest more happening than just a Chorus passing on information

- the Chorus opens quite passionately (4/3, F #1-2), but as speech turns to praise of the 'Worlds best Garden he achieved' so intellect begins to take over (6/3, F #3)

- and, interestingly, considering the content of loss, the succession of Henry's son plus the losses are handled almost totally intellectually (11/1, F #4 till the last line and a half of the speech), a case of the Chorus holding the tongue perhaps?

- yet in the final appeal to the audience for acceptance of this and the 'Henry The Sixt' cycle finishes slightly emotional (0/1, the last line and a half of the speech)

Griffith

Well, the voyce goes Madam,
between 4.2.11 - 30

Background: Wolsey has been commanded by the King to hand over the Great Seal, and then 'to Confine your selfe/To Asher-house, my Lord of Winchesters' to await the King's pleasure. However, as ex-Queene Katherine's man Griffith reports, things turned out somewhat differently.

Style: as part of a three-handed scene

Where: the Queene's personal chambers

To Whom: ex-Queene Katherine, in front of her woman Patience

Take Note: Despite the overall self control throughout the speech (21/14 overall), Griffith seems somewhat emotional at certain points in recounting the death of Wolsey, Katherine's old adversary.

Griffith

1   Well, the voice goes, madam :
     For after the stout Earl Northumberland
     Arrested him at York, and brought him forward,
     As a man sorely tainted, to his answer,
     He fell sick suddenly and grew so ill
     He could not sit his mule .

---

2   At last, with easy [roads], he came to Leicester,
     Lodg'd in the abbey ; where the reverend abbot
     With all his [convent], honorably receiv'd him ;
     To whom he gave these words : "O father abbot,
     An old man, broken with the storms of state,
     Is come to lay his weary bones among ye ;
     Give him a little earth for charity ! "

3   So went to bed ; where eagerly his sickness
     Pursu'd him still, and three nights after this,
     About the hour of eight, which he himself
     Foretold should be his last, full of repentance,
     Continual meditations, tears, and sorrows,
     He gave his honors to the world again,
     His blessed part to heaven, and slept in peace .

Griffith

1   Well, the voyce goes Madam,
    For after the stout Earle Northumberland
    Arrested him at Yorke, and brought him forward
    As a man sorely tainted, to his Answer,
    He fell sicke sodainly, and grew so ill
    He could not sit his Mule .

---

2   At last, with easie [Rodes], he came to Leicester,
    Lodg'd in the Abbey ; where the reverend Abbot
    With all his [Covent], honourably receiv'd him ;
    To whom he gave these words .

3   O Father Abbot,
    An old man, broken with the stormes of State,
    Is come to lay his weary bones among ye :
    Give him a little earth for Charity .

4   So went to bed ;where eagerly his sicknesse
    Pursu'd him still, and three nights after this,
    About the houre of eight, which he himselfe
    Foretold should be his last, full of Repentance,
    Continuall Meditations, Teares, and Sorrowes,
    He gave his Honors to the world agen,
    His blessed part to Heaven, and slept in peace .

- the speech starts passionately (6/5, F #1) as Griffith recounts Wolsey's arrest and ensuing sickness

- and though the description of Wolsey's journey to Leicester Abbey is strongly intellectual (5/1, F #2), the two semicolons suggest that for some reason Griffith is having difficulty in controlling himself as he describes the moment of arrival and Wolsey's first words

- this is heightened in that while most modern texts add what was said to the same sentence (mt. #2), while F's Griffith has to take control of himself via a new sentence (F # 3) which he does (4/1) before quoting Wolsey's words of humility

- then, for a moment, self-control disappears as Griffith builds to an emotional description (0/3, the first three and a half lines of F #4), describing the hour Wolsey 'Foretold' would be his last: the build starts in a surprising way, with a monosyllabic unembellished sur-round phrase, ending with an (emotional) semicolon - perhaps Griffith is already moved by what he is about to say and has to control himself before continuing

- and Griffith finishes passionately (6/3, the end of F #4) as he gener-ously describes Wolsey's death

BIBLIOGRAPHY

AND

APPENDICES

The most easily accessible general information is to be found under the citations of *Campbell,* and of *Halliday.* The finest summation of matters academic is to be found within the all-encompassing *A Textual Companion,* listed below in the first part of the bibliography under *Wells, Stanley and Taylor, Gary* (eds.)

Individual modern editions consulted are listed below under the separate headings 'The Complete Works in Compendium Format' and 'The Complete Works in Separate Individual Volumes,' from which the modern text audition speeches have been collated and compiled.

All modern act, scene, and/or line numbers refer the reader to *The Riverside Shakespeare,* in my opinion still the best of the complete works, despite the excellent compendiums that have been published since.

The F/Q material is taken from a variety of already published sources, including not only all the texts listed in the 'Photostatted Reproductions in Compendium Format' below, but also earlier individually printed volumes, such as the twentieth century editions published under the collective title *The Facsimiles of Plays from The First Folio of Shakespeare* by Faber & Gwyer, and the nineteenth century editions published on behalf of The New Shakespere Society.

The heading 'Single Volumes of Special Interest' is offered to newcomers to Shakespeare in the hope that the books may add useful knowledge about the background and craft of this most fascinating of theatrical figures.

PHOTOSTATTED REPRODUCTIONS OF THE ORIGINAL TEXTS IN COMPENDIUM FORMAT

Allen, M.J.B. and K. Muir, (eds.). *Shakespeare's Plays in Quarto.* Berkeley: University of California Press, 1981.

Blaney, Peter (ed.). *The Norton Facsimile (The First Folio of Shakespeare).* New York: W.W.Norton & Co., Inc., 1996 (see also Hinman, below).

Brewer D.S. (ed.). *Mr. William Shakespeare's Comedies, Histories & Tragedies, The Second/Third/Fourth Folio Reproduced in Facsimile.* (3 vols.), 1983.

Hinman, Charlton (ed.). *The Norton Facsimile (The First Folio of Shake-speare)*. New York: W.W.Norton & Company, Inc., 1968.

Kokeritz, Helge (ed.). *Mr. William Shakespeare 's Comedies, Histories & Tragedies*. New Haven: Yale University Press, 1954.

Moston, Doug (ed.). *Mr. William Shakespeare's Comedies, Histories, and Tragedies*. New York: Routledge, 1998.

MODERN TYPE VERSION OF THE FIRST FOLIO IN COMPENDIUM FORMAT

Freeman, Neil. (ed.). *The Applause First Folio of Shakespeare in Modern Type*. New York & London: Applause Books, 2001.

MODERN TEXT VERSIONS OF THE COMPLETE WORKS IN COMPENDIUM FORMAT

Craig, H. and D. Bevington (eds.). *The Complete Works of Shakespeare*. Glenview: Scott, Foresman and Company, 1973.

Evans, G.B. (ed.). *The Riverside Shakespeare*. Boston: Houghton Mifflin Company, 1974.

Wells, Stanley and Gary Taylor (eds.). *The Oxford Shakespeare, William Shakespeare , the Complete Works, Original Spelling Edition,* Oxford: The Clarendon Press, 1986.

Wells, Stanley and Gary Taylor (eds.). *The Oxford Shakespeare, William Shakespeare, The Complete Works, Modern Spelling Edition*. Oxford: The Clarendon Press, 1986.

MODERN TEXT VERSIONS OF THE COMPLETE WORKS IN SEPARATE INDIVIDUAL VOLUMES

The Arden Shakespeare. London: Methuen & Co. Ltd., Various dates, editions, and editors .

Folio Texts. Freeman, Neil H. M. (ed.) Applause First Folio Editions, 1997, and following.

The New Cambridge Shakespeare. Cambridge: Cambridge University Press. Various dates, editions, and editors.

New Variorum Editions of Shakespeare. Furness, Horace Howard (original editor.). New York: 1880, Various reprints. All these volumes have been in a state of re-editing and reprinting since they first appeared in 1880. Various dates, editions, and editors.

The Oxford Shakespeare. Wells, Stanley (general editor). Oxford: Oxford University Press, Various dates and editors.

The New Penguin Shakespeare . Harmondsworth, Middlesex: Penguin Books, Various dates and editors.

The Shakespeare Globe Acting Edition. Tucker, Patrick and Holden, Michael. (eds.). London: M.H.Publications, Various dates.

SINGLE VOLUMES OF SPECIAL INTEREST

Baldwin, T.W. *William Shakespeare's Petty School.* 1943.

Baldwin, T.W. *William Shakespeare's Small wtin and Lesse Greeke.* (2 vols.) 1944.

Barton, John. *Playing Shakespeare.* 1984.

Beckerman, Bernard. *Shakespeare at the Globe, I 599-1609.* 1962. Berryman, John. *Berryman's Shakespeare.* 1999.

Bloom, Harold. *Shakespeare: The Invention of the Human.* 1998. Booth, Stephen (ed.). *Shakespeare's Sonnets.* 1977.

Briggs, Katharine. *An Encyclopedia of Fairies.* 1976.

Campbell, Oscar James, and Edward G. Quinn (eds.). *The Reader's Encyclopedia of Shakespeare. 1966.*

Crystal, David, and Ben Crystal. *Shakespeare's Words: A Glossary & Language Companion.* 2002.

Flatter, Richard. *Shakespeare's Producing Hand.* 1948 (reprint).

Ford, Boris. (ed.). *The Age of Shakespeare.* 1955.

Freeman, Neil H.M. *Shakespeare's First Texts.* 1994.

Greg, W.W. *The Editorial Problem in Shakespeare: A Survey of the Foundations of the Text.* 1954 (3rd. edition).

Gurr, Andrew . *Playgoing in Shakespeare's London.* 1987. Gurr, Andrew. *The Shakespearean Stage, 1574-1642.* 1987. Halliday, F.E. *A Shakespeare Companion.* 1952.

Harbage, Alfred. *Shakespeare's Audience.* 1941.

Harrison, G.B. (ed.). *The Elizabethan Journals.* 1965 (revised, 2 vols.).

Harrison, G.B. (ed.). *A Jacobean Journal.* 1941.

Harrison, G.B. (ed.). *A Second Jacobean Journal.* 1958.

Hinman, Charlton. *The Printing and Proof Reading of the First Folio of Shakespeare.* 1963 (2 vols.).

Joseph, Bertram. *Acting Shakespeare.* 1960.

Joseph, Miriam (Sister). *Shakespeare's Use of The Arts of wnguage.* 1947.

King, T.J. *Casting Shakespeare's Plays.* 1992.

Lee, Sidney and C.T. Onions. *Shakespeare's England : An Account Of The Life And Manners Of His Age.* (2 vols.) 1916.

Linklater, Kristin. *Freeing Shakespeare's Voice*. 1992.

Mahood, **M .M.** *Shakespeare's Wordplay*. 1957.

O'Connor, Gary. *William Shakespeare: A Popular Life*. 2000.

Ordish, T.F. *Early London Theatres*. 1894. (1971 reprint).

Rodenberg, Patsy. *Speaking Shakespeare*. 2002.

Schoenbaum. S. *William Shakespeare: A Documentary Life*. 1975.

Shapiro, Michael. *Children of the Revels*. 1977.

Simpson, Percy. *Shakespeare's Punctuation*. 1969 (reprint).

Smith, Irwin. *Shakespeare's Blackfriars Playhouse* . 1964.

Southern, Richard. *The Staging of Plays Before Shakespeare*. 1973.

Spevack, M. *A Complete and Systematic Concordance to the Works Of Shakespeare* . 1968-1980 (9vols.).

Tillyard, E.M.W. *The Elizabethan World Picture*. 1942.

Trevelyan, G.M. (ed.). *Illustrated English Social History*. 1942.

Vendler, Helen. *The Art of Shakespeare's Sonnets*. 1999.

Walker, Alice F. *Textual Problems of the First Folio*. 1953.

Walton, J.K. *The Quarto Copy of the First Folio*. 1971.

Warren, Michael. *William Shakespeare, The Parallel King Lear 1608-1623*.

Wells, Stanley and Taylor, Gary (eds.). *Modernising Shakespeare's Spelling, with Three Studies in The Text of Henry V.* 1975.

Wells, Stanley. *Re-Editing Shakespeare for the Modern Reader.* 1984.

Wells, Stanley and Gary Taylor (eds.). *William Shakespeare: A Textual Companion* . 1987.

Wright, George T. *Shakespeare's Metrical Art.* 1988.

HISTORICAL DOCUMENTS

Daniel, Samuel. *The Fowre Bookes of the Civile Warres Between The Howses Of Lancaster and Yorke.* 1595.

Holinshed, Raphael. *Chronicles of England, Scotland and Ireland.* 1587 (2nd. edition).

Halle, Edward. *The Union of the Two Noble and Illustre Famelies of Lancastre And Yorke.* 1548 (2nd. edition).

Henslowe, Philip: Foakes, R.A. and Rickert (eds.). *Henslowe's Diary.* 1961.

Plutarch: North, Sir Thomas (translation of a work in French prepared by Jacques Amyots). *The Lives of The Noble Grecians and Romanes.* 1579.

APPENDIX 1:
GUIDE TO THE EARLY TEXTS

A QUARTO (Q)

A single text, so called because of the book size resulting from a particular method of printing. Eighteen of Shakespeare's plays were published in this format by different publishers at various dates between 1594-1622, prior to the appearance of the 1623 Folio.

THE FIRST FOLIO (F1)'

Thirty-six of Shakespeare's plays (excluding *Pericles* and *Two Noble Kinsmen,* in which he had a hand) appeared in one volume, published in 1623. All books of this size were termed Folios, again because of the sheet size and printing method, hence this volume is referred to as the First Folio. For publishing details see Bibliography, 'Photostated Reproductions of the Original Texts.'

THE SECOND FOLIO (F2)

Scholars suggest that the Second Folio, dated 1632 but perhaps not published until 1640, has little authority, especially since it created hundreds of new problematic readings of its own. Nevertheless more than 800 modern text readings can be attributed to it. The **Third Folio** (1664) and the **Fourth Folio** (1685) have even less authority, and are rarely consulted except in cases of extreme difficulty.

APPENDIX 2:
WORD, WORDS, WORDS

PART ONE: VERBAL CONVENTIONS (AND HOW THEY WILL BE SET IN THE FOLIO TEXT)

"THEN" AND "THAN"

These two words, though their neutral vowels sound different to modern ears, were almost identical to Elizabethan speakers and readers, despite their different meanings. F and Q make little distinction between them, setting them interchangeably . The original setting will be used, and the modern reader should soon get used to substituting one for the other as necessary.

"I," "AY," AND "AYE"

F/Q often print the personal pronoun "I" and the word of agreement "aye" simply as "I." Again, the modern reader should quickly get used to this and make the substitution when necess ary. The reader should also be aware that very occasionally either word could be used and the phrase make perfect sense, even though different meanings would be implied.

"MY SELFE/HIM SELFE/HER SELFE" VERSUS "MYSELF/HIMSELF/HER-SELF"

Generally F/Q separate the two parts of the word, "my selfe" while most modern texts set the single word "myself." The difference is vital, based on Elizabethan philosophy. Elizabethans regarded themselves as composed of two parts, the corporeal "I," and the more spiritual part, the "self." Thus, when an Elizabethan character refers to "my selfe," he or she is often referring to what is to all intents and purposes a separate being, even if that being is a particular part of him- or herself. Thus soliloquies can be thought of as a debate between the "I" and "my selfe," and, in such speeches, even though there may be only one character on-stage, it's as if there were two distinct entities present.

UNUSUAL SPELLING OF REAL NAMES, BOTH OF PEOPLE AND PLACES

Real names, both of people and places, and foreign languages are often reworked for modern understanding. For example, the French town often set in Fl as "Callice" is usually reset as "Calais." F will be set as is.

NON-GRAMMATICAL USES OF VERBS IN BOTH TENSE AND APPLICATION

Modern texts 'correct' the occasional Elizabethan practice of setting a singular noun with plural verb (and vice versa), as well as the infrequent use of the past tense of a verb to describe a current situation. The F reading will be set as is, without annotation.

ALTERNATIVE SETTINGS OF A WORD WHERE DIFFERENT SPELLINGS MAINTAIN THE SAME MEANING

F/Q occasionally set what appears to modern eyes as an archaic spelling of a word for which there is a more common modern alternative, for example "murther" for murder , "burthen" for burden, "moe" for more, "vilde" for vile. Though some modern texts set the Fl (or alternative Q) setting, others modernise. Fl will be set as is with no annotation.

ALTERNATIVE SETTINGS OF A WORD WHERE DIFFERENT SPELLINGS SUGGEST DIFFERENT MEANINGS

Far more complicated is the situation where, while an Elizabethan could substitute one word formation for another and still imply the same thing, to modern eyes the substituted word has an entirely different meaning to the one it has replaced. The following is by no means an exclusive list of the more common dual-spelling, dual-meaning words

anticke-antique	mad-made	sprite-spirit
born-borne	metal-mettle	sun-sonne
hart-heart	mote-moth	travel-travaill
human-humane	pour-(po wre)-power	through-thorough
lest-least	reverent-reverend	troth-truth
lose-loose	right-rite	whether-whither

Some of these doubles offer a metrical problem too, for example "sprite," a one syllable word, versus "spirit." A potential problem occurs in *A Midsummer Nights Dream,* where the modern text s set Q1's "thorough," and thus the scansion pattern of elegant magic can be established, whereas F1's more plebeian "through" sets up a much more awkward and clumsy moment.

The F reading will be set in the Folio Text, as will the modern texts' substitution of a different word formation in the Modern Text. If the modern text substitution has the potential to alter the meaning (and sometimes scansion) of the line, it will be noted accordingly.

PART TWO: WORD FORMATIONS COUNTED AS EQUIVALENTS FOR THE FOLLOWING SPEECHES

Often the spelling differences between the original and modern texts are quite obvious, as with "she"/"shee". And sometimes Folio text passages are so flooded with longer (and sometimes shorter) spellings that, as described in the General Introduction, it would seem that vocally something unusual is taking place as the character speaks.

However, there are some words where the spelling differences are so marginal that they need not be explored any further. The following is by no mean s an exclusive list of word s that in the main will not be taken into account when discussing emotional moments in the various commentaries accompanying the audition speeches.

(modern text spelling shown first)

and- &	murder - murther	tabor - taber
apparent - apparant	mutinous - mutenous	ta'en - tane
briars - briers	naught - nought	then - than
choice - choise	obey - obay	theater - theatre
defense - defence	o'er - o're	uncurrant - uncurrent
debtor - debter	offense - offence	than - then
enchant - inchant	quaint - queint	venomous - venemous
endurance - indurance	reside - recide	virtue - vertue
ere - e'er	Saint - S.	weight - waight
expense - expence	sense - sence	
has - ha's	sepulchre - sepulcher	
heinous - hainous	show - shew	
1'11 - Ile	solicitor - soliciter	
increase - encrease	sugar - suger	

APPENDIX 3:
THE PATTERN OF MAGIC, RITUAL *&*
INCANTATION

THE PATTERNS OF "NORMAL" CONVERSATION

The normal pattern of a regular Shakespearean verse line is akin to five pairs of human heart beats, with ten syllables being arranged in five pairs of beats, each pair alternating a pattern of a weak stress followed by a strong stress. Thus, a normal ten syllable heartbeat line (with the emphasis on the capitalised words) would read as

weak- STRONG, weak - STRONG, weak- STRONG, weak- STRONG, weak- STRONG
(shall   I   com-   PARE thee   TO   a   SUMM- ers DAY)

Breaks would either be in length (under or over ten syllables) or in rhythm (any combinations of stresses other than the five pairs of weak-strong as shown above), or both together.

THE PATTERNS OF MAGIC, RITUAL, AND INCANTATION

Whenever magic is used in the Shakespeare plays the form of the spoken verse changes markedly in two ways . The length is usually reduced from ten to just seven syllables, and the pattern of stresses is completely reversed, as if the heartbeat was being forced either by the circumstances of the scene or by the need of the speaker to completely change direction. Thus in comparison to the normal line shown above, or even the occasional minor break, the more tortured and even dangerous magic or ritual line would read as

STRONG - weak, STRONG- weak, STRONG - weak, STRONG
(WHEN   shall   WE   three   MEET   a   GAINE)

The strain would be even more severely felt in an extended passage, as when the three weyward Sisters begin the potion that will fetch Macbeth to them. Again, the spoken emphasis is on the capitalised words and the effort of, and/or fixed determination in, speaking can clearly be felt.

> THRICE the BRINDed CAT hath MEW"D
> THRICE and ONCE the HEDGE-Pigge WHIN"D
> HARPier CRIES, 'tis TIME, 'tis TIME.

UNUSUAL ASPECTS OF MAGIC

It's not always easy for the characters to maintain it. And the magic doesn't always come when the character expects it. What is even more interesting is that while the pattern is found a lot in the Comedies, it is usually in much gentler situations, often in songs *(Two Gentlemen of Verona, Merry Wives of Windsor, Much Ado About Nothing, Twelfth Night, The Winters Tale)* and/or simplistic poetry *(Loves Labours Lost* and *As You Like It),* as well as the casket sequence in *The Merchant of Venice.*

It's too easy to dismiss these settings as inferior poetry known as doggerel. But this may be doing the moment and the character a great disservice. The language may be simplistic, but the passion and the magical/ritual intent behind it is wonderfully sincere. It's not just a matter of magic for the sake of magic, as with Pucke and Oberon enchanting mortals and Titania. It's a matter of the human heart's desires too. Orlando, in *As You Like It,* when writing peons of praise to Rosalind suggesting that she is composed of the best parts of the mythical heroines because

> THEREfore HEAVen NATure CHARG"D
> THAT one B0Die SHOULD be FILL"D
> WITH all GRACes WIDE enLARG"D

And what could be better than Autolycus *(The Winters Tale)* using magic in his opening song as an extra enticement to trap the unwary into buying all his peddler's goods, ballads, and trinkets.

To help the reader, most magic/ritual lines will be bolded in the Folio text version of the speeches.

ACKNOWLEDGMENTS

Neil dedicated *The Applause First Folio in Modern Type*
      "To All Who Have Gone Before"
and there are so many who have gone before in the sharing of Shakespeare through publication. Back to John Heminge and Henry Condell who published *Mr. William Shakespeares Comedies, Histories, & Tragedies* which we now know as The First Folio and so preserved 18 plays of Shakespeare which might otherwise have been lost. As they wrote in their note "To the great Variety of Readers.":

> Reade him, therefore; and againe, and againe : And if then you doe not like him, surely you are in some manifest danger, not to understand him. And so we leave you to other of his Friends, whom if you need, can be your guides: if you neede them not, you can lead yourselves, and others, and such readers we wish him.

I want to thank John Cerullo for believing in these books and helping to spread Neil's vision. I want to thank Rachel Reiss for her invaluable advice and assistance. I want to thank my wife, Maren and my family for giving me support, but above all I want to thank Julie Stockton, Neil's widow, who was able to retrive Neil's files from his old non-internet connected Mac, without which these books would not be possible. Thank you Julie.

Shakespeare for Everyone!

Paul Sugarman, April 2021

AUTHOR BIOS

Neil Freeman (1941-2015) trained as an actor at the Bristol Old Vic Theatre School. In the world of professional Shakespeare he acted in fourteen of the plays, directed twenty-four, and coached them all many times over.

His groundbreaking work in using the first printings of the Shakespeare texts in performance, on the rehearsal floor and in the classroom led to lectures at the Shakespeare Association of America and workshops at both the ATHE and VASTA, and grants/fellowships from the National Endowment for the Arts (USA), The Social Science and Humanities Research Council (Canada), and York University in Toronto. He prepared and annotated the thirty-six individual Applause First Folio editions of Shakespeare's plays and the complete *The Applause First Folio of Shakespeare in Modern Type*. For Applause he also compiled *Once More Unto the Speech, Dear Friends*, three volumes (Comedy, History and Tragedy) of Shakespeare speeches with commentary and insights to inform audition preparation.

He was Professor Emeritus in the Department of Theatre, Film and Creative Writing at the University of British Columbia, and dramaturg with The Savage God project, both in Vancouver, Canada. He also taught regularly at the National Theatre School of Canada, Concordia University, Brigham Young University.. He had a Founder's Ring (and the position of Master Teacher) with Shakespeare & Company in Lenox, Mass: he was associated with the Will Geer Theatre in Los Angeles; Bard on the Beach in Vancouver; Repercussion Theatre in Montreal; and worked with the Stratford Festival, Canada, and Shakespeare Santa Cruz.

Paul Sugarman is an actor, editor, writer, and teacher of Shakespeare. He is founder of the Instant Shakespeare Company, which has presented annual readings of all of Shakespeare's plays in New York City for over twenty years. For Applause Theatre & Cinema Books, he edited John Russell Brown's publication of *Shakescenes: Shakespeare for Two* and The Applause Shakespeare Library, as well as Neil Freeman's Applause First Folio Editions and *The Applause First Folio of Shakespeare in Modern Type*. He has published pocket editions of all of Shakespeare's plays using the original settings of the First Folio in modern type for Puck Press. Sugarman studied with Kristin Linklater and Tina Packer at Shakespeare & Company where he met Neil Freeman.